THE GREATEST SECRET

Rhonda Byrne

HarperOne
An Imprint of HarperCollins*Publishers*

HarperCollins books may be purchased for educational, business, or sales promotional use. For information, please email the Special Markets Department at SPsales@harpercollins.com.

FIRST EDITION

Creative direction and artwork by Nic George
Graphic art and design by Josh Hedlund
Book layout by Yvonne Chan

Library of Congress Cataloging-in-Publication Data has been applied for.

ISBN 978-0-06307848-2

20 21 22 23 24 RTL 10 9 8 7 6 5 4 3 2 1

Dedicated to all of humanity

May The Greatest Secret *free you from all suffering
and bring you everlasting happiness.*

That is my intention for you, and for every human being.

"Of all the things human beings can learn
in this life, I have the greatest news to tell you,
the most beautiful thing to share . . ."
—Mooji

Contents

Acknowledgments

The Greatest Secret could not have come into the world without the help and support of many. First, I wish to acknowledge and honor the teachers whose illuminating teachings are featured throughout this book. They epitomize grace and wisdom, and I am beyond grateful for their presence and willingness to be a part of this life-transforming book.

To the scientists and doctors featured in this book, my deepest gratitude for your leading-edge perspectives that humankind needs to take us out of the dark ages of old paradigms that don't work anymore and into the illuminating presence of the true Infinite Being that we are.

To the members of The Secret team who worked with me on *The Greatest Secret*, there are no words that can describe my gratitude for your dedication and support of this project. Whenever I announce to the team that I have discovered something earth-shattering that I must share with the world, I am sure they take a deep breath, wondering what is going to come next. But without exception, they open their minds and lift their consciousness to the level that is required, so as to provide their invaluable contribution through their roles.

Skye Byrne (my daughter) is The Secret's editor, my editor, and my human compass for all of my books. To edit my books, Skye needs to understand all the teachings at the highest possible level to ensure that I stay on track and fulfill my greatest desire—to write as simply as possible so that millions will be set free from suffering and be in joy. To work on the early stages of a book is no mean feat, and there isn't another person on the planet who could do it to the level of brilliance and perfection with which she does it. To Skye comes my deepest and immeasurable gratitude, as her guiding hand can be found on every page.

Another hand you will find on every page is that of our creative director, Nic George. The beautiful design of this book is due to his extraordinary creative abilities, his beautiful creative eye and hand, and his deep intuitive sense. Creating a new book with Nic is a process of sheer joy, and I am blessed to have him, along with Josh Hedland, who worked side by side with Nic on the cover and interior of *The Greatest Secret*.

Glenda Bell worked diligently with the teachers, contributors, and their teams so that the teachings would be accurately portrayed in the book. In a mighty effort, she worked selflessly and enthusiastically around the clock, through the nights and weekends, to connect with all time zones, for which I am very grateful.

Thank you to the rest of the amazing Secret team: Don Zyck, our CFO, who is always ready for the next quantum leap with our company and who ushers us through the legal and financial requirements, keeping everything flowing toward our intention; Josh Gold, who manages all of our social media platforms brilliantly and who will ensure that every country in the world knows of this book; Marcy Koltun-Crilley, my dearest friend who has been on this journey with me from the beginning and who I am honored to say is an integral part of The Secret team; and producer Paul Harrington, who has been with me since a decade before The Secret even came into being. Paul encouraged and inspired me to write *The Greatest Secret* in the early stages, when it seemed almost impossible that this precious truth could be conveyed simply. Paul also produced *The Greatest Secret* audiobook, working beside Tim Patterson in post-production and bringing the revelatory words in this book to life in audio form.

My gratitude to the amazing HarperCollins team, whose excitement in working on this book is contagious. Thank you to the wonderful Judith Curr, president and publisher of HarperOne, and my fantastic editor, Gideon Weil, who were both such a joy to work with. Thank you also to Brian Murray, Terri Leonard, Yvonne Chan, Suzanne Quist, Laina Adler, Edward Benitez, Aly Mostel, Melinda Mullin, Adrian Morgan, Dwight Been, Anna Brower, Lucile Culver, and Rosie Black.

Thank you to the international HarperCollins team: Chantal Restivo-Alessi, Emily Martin, Juliette Shapland, Catherine Barbosa-Ross, and Julianna Wojcik. Thank you to the HarperCollins UK team: Charlie Redmayne, Kate Elton, Oliver Malcolm, Katya Shipster, Helen Rochester, Simon Gerratt, and Julie MacBrayne. And thank you to the HarperCollins Global Publishing Partners: Brasil, Espanol, Mexico, Iberica, Italia, Holland, France, Germany, Polska, Japan, and Nordic.

Special thanks to the following people who helped me with their invaluable feedback: Peter Foyo, Kim Wall, John Wall, Hannah Hodgden, Marcy Koltun-Crilley, Mark Weaver, and Fred Nalder.

To my family, Peter Byrne, Oku Den, Kevin (Kid) McKemy, Henley McKemy, Savannah Byrne Cronin, and my daughter Hayley, who was the force that set me on my incredible journey in search of the truth sixteen years ago. To my dearest sisters, Pauline Vernon, Glenda Bell, and Jan Child, thank you for loving me and for allowing me to love you.

And finally, thank you to my amazing and beautiful teacher, whose words and teachings of the truth over the past four years have radically transformed my life and helped me to see clearly who I really am. This precious book is in your hands because of her unlimited giving and her patience in helping direct me home. My love for her knows no boundary.

...ment of a ... sure and yet ...most...

...ster... for one of delusion in de...
...little your mind can't understand it... so
...don't believe it... so good you can't accept it... more
...the most concealed... is the greatest discovery a
...thing... is all... hidden in plain sight... more hidden
...the most concealed... more evident than the most evident of
...clearer... with... greater than the... greatest secret is
...easy for every one of us to see... leaves it at the
...door... yet so... our mind can't... unputdownable peace...
...of our emotional and mental turmoil has ceased. The fear...
...ness... the ... truth gives you... over everything... the
...the m... it bring the most of experience and yet the
...overlooked... the secret of secrets... The end of del... ...is
...you can see it... is subtle your mind can't... stand it...
...simple you can't believe it... so good you can't accept it...
...hidden than the most concealed... this is the greatest...
...a human being can make... hidden in...
...den than the most concealed... more...
...evident... things... there's nothing greater...
...plainly in plain view for... any one o...

...The most obvious element of experience ...

...overlooked... the secret of secrets... the end of delusion... is that

you can't see it... so subtle your mind can't understand it...

simple you can't believe it... so good you can't ... it ...

hidden that the most ... hidden... this is the greatest ...

human being can make... hidden in plain sight... more ...

than the most concealed... more evident than the most obvious

thing... there's nothing greater... there's ...

...

...

...

...

...the most ... element of experience ...

...overlooked... the secret of secrets... the end of delusion...

lose you... t see it... so subtle your mind can't understand...

so simple you can't believe it... so good you can't accept...

more hidden than the most concealed... this is the greatest

...man being ... can make... hidden in plain ...

...the most concealed... more evident...

...there's nothing greater... on the ...

...plain sight... for every one of us ...

The Beginning

After the release of *The Secret* in 2006, my life became what I can only describe as a dream life. Through practicing *The Secret* principles religiously, my mind had become predominantly positive, and so my life reflected that positive state in my happiness, health, relationships, and finances. I also found myself with a natural love and gratitude for everything in life.

But despite all of that, something inside me continued to urge me on to seek more of the truth; something propelled me to continue my search, though for what, I didn't yet know.

Unbeknownst to me at the time, I had begun what was to become a ten-year journey! It started with studying the teachings of an ancient tradition in Europe, the Rose Cross Order, and I studied their profound teachings for many years. I also spent some years studying Buddhism, the many works of the Christian mystics, theology, Hinduism, Taoism, and Sufism. After I studied the ancient traditions and their historical teachings, my search turned back toward the present time, and I started following recent teachers like J. Krishnamurti, Robert Adams, Lester Levenson, and Ramana Maharshi, as well as some teachers still living today.

Throughout my journey I learned many things that are unknown to the public at large, and while they were fascinating, none of them made me feel that I had found *the* truth.

As the years passed by, I even considered that searching might be my life forevermore. I didn't realize it then, but I was looking for the truth in the world, when all along it was closer to me than I could ever have imagined.

Ten years after my search began, in early January of 2016, a challenging situation arose in my life that caused me to feel deep disappointment. I was surprised at the depth of negative emotion that I felt. How could I feel so bad when I usually felt so good? But that disappointing situation was to become the greatest gift in my search for the truth.

To turn my disappointment around, I grabbed my iPad and watched an interview on Conscious TV with a man called David Bingham. At the time of the interview David was not a teacher but was just an ordinary everyday person like you and me, with one difference: after twenty years of searching, he had discovered the truth!

I watched the interview, and afterward I listened to a podcast that David recommended. I listened intently to the podcast, and during it I heard that most people overlook this discovery—not because it's difficult, but because it's so simple. Then, I was able to speak with David on the phone, and during our conversation he said, "Look at what I'm pointing to. It's right here." And suddenly I saw what I had been searching for. It *was* so simple, and it *was* right here. Just like that—after ten years—my search ended! I can say without any hesitation that the happiness and joy I felt from this discovery was worth every second of my years-long journey. Even if it had taken my entire life to discover it, it would have been worth it.

In the end, just one simple discovery was the whole truth that I had been looking for, which is actually what everyone is looking for, whether they realize it or not. And once I had seen the truth, I could see that it was everywhere. Everything I had been reading and learning for ten years contained it; I just didn't have the eyes to see it at that time. I had been searching for years, from one tradition and philosophy to the next, and what I had been looking for had been right in front of me all along!

From the moment I made the discovery, I knew that there was nothing more important than to understand this discovery more, live it completely, and then share it with the world. My hope was to show the way out for those experiencing hardship, to help end the pain and suffering that so many are enduring, and to shine a light to a future where we can live without anxiety or fear.

I had already been putting notes from everything I was learning in a folder on my computer that was entitled "My Next Book." It was an intuitive sense that inspired me to record everything I was discovering, in the hope that I could eventually share it with the world. Those cherished notes, when I had finished collating them, became the foundation of this book.

Just two months after discovering the truth through David Bingham, I met someone else who was to have an enormous effect on my life, and on the creation of this book. She walked into a room I was in at a retreat, and when I walked up to talk to her, her presence had such a profound effect on me that any trace of negativity from my entire life was gone in an instant! She had been a student of one of my all-time favorite teachers, the late Robert Adams. I knew instantly that she was my teacher, the one who would help me fully realize and live the truth in this lifetime, and she has remained my teacher for the past four years. Her teachings are straightforward, beautifully simple, and she never hesitates to tell me if I'm going in the wrong direction. While her name remains anonymous at her request, I have shared many of her life-changing teachings that propelled my life into one of constant joy and happiness. My deepest wish is that they will do the same for you.

She, along with the other teachers featured in this book, helped lead me out of the darkness of ignorance by illuminating this one discovery. Every one of them helped me to understand the truth that I had discovered more deeply and to live from it more fully, and the love I feel for them is infinite. Their words that changed my life forever are featured throughout this book.

With every step you take through this book, you will become happier and your life will become more effortless, and that happiness and effortlessness will continue to increase without any end. Any fear and uncertainty of the future will no longer plague you. Any anxiety and stress about your daily struggles or world events will dissolve. You can be free of every form of suffering that you might be experiencing right now. And you will be.

While there are certainly some huge revelations throughout these pages, there are also many simple practices to immediately put those revelations into practice. The practices alone are worth their weight in gold. I know. I am the living proof of how well they work.

The Secret showed you how to create anything you want to be, do, or have. Nothing has changed—it is as true today as it ever was. This book reveals the greatest discovery a human being can ever make and shows you the way out of negativity, problems, and what you don't want, to a life of permanent happiness and bliss.

It simply doesn't get any better than this. It is my greatest joy to welcome you to *The Greatest Secret*.

HIDDEN IN PLAIN SIGHT

Of the billions of people on our planet, only a few have discovered the truth. Those few are completely free from the turmoil and negativity of life and live in permanent peace and happiness. For the rest of us, whether we realize it or not, we've been in search of this truth unceasingly every single day of our lives.

Despite the fact that this great secret has been written about and alluded to by many great sages, prophets, and religious leaders throughout history, the majority of us still remain ignorant of the single greatest discovery we can ever make. Among those who have shared this discovery with us are Buddha, Krishna, Lao Tzu, Jesus Christ, Yogananda, Krishnamurti, and the Dalai Lama.

While they each have different teachings that were appropriate for their time, they all refer to the same truth—the truth about us and the truth behind our world.

"In some religions this truth is expressed less openly and clearly than in others, but it is nevertheless the truth that lies at the heart of every religion."
Michael James, from Happiness and the Art of Being

This great secret is in plain view for every one of us to see. It's closer to us than our very breath, yet we've missed it! Ancient traditions knew that to hide a secret it should be put in plain sight, where no one will think to look for it. And that's exactly where The Greatest Secret lies.

"Thus it is referred to in the Kashmir Shaivite tradition as 'the greatest secret, more hidden than the most concealed and yet more evident than the most evident of things.'"
Rupert Spira, from Being Aware of Being Aware

We've missed the truth for thousands of years because we've not looked at what is right in front of us. We've become easily distracted by our problems, the drama in our lives, the comings and goings of the events in the world, and we've missed the greatest discovery we can make that is right here before us—a discovery that can take us out of suffering and into lasting happiness.

What secret can possibly be so life-changing? What single discovery can ever end suffering, or bring everlasting peace and happiness?

Quite simply, a secret that reveals who you really are.

You might think you know who you are, but if you think you're an individual person with a name, who's a certain age, from a particular race, who has a profession, a family history, and various life experiences, you will be stunned by the revelation of who you *really* are.

"The only way that someone can be of help to you is by challenging your ideas."
Anthony de Mello, S.J., from Awareness: Conversations with the Masters

We've all accepted many false ideas and beliefs throughout our lives, and those false ideas and beliefs have kept us enslaved. We've been told that there's limitation and lack in the world—that there's not enough money, time, resources, love, or health: "Life is short," "You're only human," "You have to work hard and struggle to get somewhere in life," "We're running out of resources," "The world is in turmoil," "The world needs saving." But the moment you see the truth, those mistruths will crumble, and your happiness will arise from the ruins.

Perhaps you're thinking, "My life is going swimmingly, and so why would I even want to know The Greatest Secret?"

To quote the wonderful late Anthony de Mello, S.J.:
"Because your life is a mess!"

You may disagree. I certainly didn't think my life was a mess either until Anthony de Mello defined exactly what he meant.

Do you ever get upset? Ever get stressed? Ever worry? Ever feel anxious, offended, or hurt? Ever feel sad, down in the dumps, or despondent? Are you ever unhappy or in a bad mood? If you experience any of these emotions at any time, then according to Anthony de Mello, your life is a mess!

You might think it's normal to be plagued by negative emotions throughout your day, but life isn't supposed to be that way. You can live your life utterly free of hurt, upset, worry, and fear, and exist in *continuous* happiness.

Life is showing us there's a way out of suffering through every single challenging circumstance we experience, especially the very challenging circumstances. But we don't see it. We're lost in our problems, and we miss the very thing that is right in front of us that is the way out of all problems forever!

"We seek happiness in experience after experience, relationship after relationship, therapy after therapy, workshop after workshop—even 'spiritual' ones, which sound so promising but never address the root cause of suffering: ignorance of our true nature."
Mooji, from White Fire, *second edition*

Whenever we suffer, it's because we've believed something about ourselves that isn't true; we've mistaken our own identity. *All* of humanity's suffering comes down to a case of mistaken identity.

The truth is, you're not a person who has no control over what happens to you and your life. You're not a person who has to slave at a job you don't like, only to die at the end of it all. You're not a person who has to struggle from paycheck to paycheck. You're not a person who needs to prove yourself or who needs anybody else's approval. The truth is, you are not really a person at all. You are most certainly having the *experience* of being a person, but in the bigger picture it's not who you are.

"It isn't the way it appears to be. You aren't what you think you are."
Jan Frazier, from The Freedom of Being

"Sometimes we're targeting the symptoms in life but the real cause in life we're missing—the understanding and recognition of our true nature. This is the one medicine for everything."
Mooji

"All the unhappiness, discontent and misery that we experience in our life is caused only by our ignorance or confused knowledge of who or what we really are. Therefore if we want to be free of all forms of misery and unhappiness, we must free ourself from our ignorance or confused knowledge of what we really are."
Michael James, from Happiness and the Art of Being

Your gauge of how your life is going is your level of happiness. How happy are you? Are you genuinely happy all of the time? Do you live within a continuous background of happiness? You're supposed to be happy all the time. Happiness *is* you. It's your true nature. It's who you really are.

"The thing that every one of us is looking for in this world is exactly the same thing. Every being, even the animals are looking for it. And what is it that we're all looking for—happiness with no sorrow. A continuous happiness with no taint whatsoever of sorrow."
Lester Levenson, from Will Power *audio*

Every action we take, every decision we make, is because we think we will be happier from it. It's not a coincidence that we're all looking for happiness; in our search for happiness, we are actually looking for ourselves without realizing it!

It's not possible to find lasting happiness through material things. Every material thing appears and eventually disappears, so if you vest your happiness in a material thing, your happiness will disappear when the material thing disappears. There's nothing wrong with material things (they are wonderful, and you deserve to have whatever you want in life), but it's a major breakthrough when you realize that you'll never find lasting happiness in them. If material things brought us happiness, then when we receive something that we really wanted, the happiness would never leave us. But it's not the case. Instead, we experience a fleeting happiness, and within a very short amount of time we're back to where we started from—a state of wanting more things in an effort to feel happy again.

There's only one way to find lasting, permanent happiness—it is to find out who you really are, because your true nature IS happiness.

"The world is so unhappy because it is ignorant of the true Self. Man's real nature is happiness. Happiness is inborn in the true Self. Man's search for happiness is an unconscious search for his true Self . . . When a man finds it, he finds a happiness which does not come to an end."
Ramana Maharshi

"The only real purpose of being here on this earth is to learn or to re-remember our original natural state of no limitations."
Lester Levenson, from Will Power *audio*

"The discovery of our true Self has the power to transform the darkness of ignorance into the light of pure understanding. It is the most profound, important and radical discovery. It is a tree that bears fruit immediately. When we realize who we are—the one experiencing and perceiving the world—so many things will be set right. There are not many things to know if truth is what you seek. It's not volumes of knowledge that are required—it's to come to the recognition of the one true Self that you are."
Mooji

Remembering who you really are has been given many names over the centuries. Enlightenment, self-realization, self-discovery, illumination, awakening, remembering. You probably think "enlightenment" can't be for you ("I'm just a normal person"), but you couldn't be further from the truth. This discovery—this happiness, this freedom—is who you are, so how can it not be for you?

"Open yourself to the possibility that you can experience *the truth* of what you are, this very moment. How, you may ask? By noticing that the only obstacle in the way is your imagination—your imagined opposition."
My teacher

"We are free, and we don't know it. It feels the furthest thing from possible, that it could be so. We'd swear we're at the mercy of what goes wrong, what goes right. And yet (here is the truth), freedom is right here."
Jan Frazier, from The Freedom of Being

"Self-realization is possible for someone who's had no education and it can also be possible for a king. There are no preconditions to self-realization. Self-realization isn't just for those who've undergone years of spiritual practice—it's possible for someone who's been drinking and smoking all the time."
David Bingham, from Conscious TV

What Will Your Life Be Like?

"I'm talking about something that hardly anyone has yet experienced. How can I describe it? No limits on anything in any direction whatsoever. The ability to do anything for the mere

thought of it. Yet it is more than that. Imagine the highest joy you can have and multiply by a hundred."
Lester Levenson, from No Attachments, No Aversions

When you fully recognize who you are, you will have a life without problems, without upset, hurt, worry, or fear. You will be free from the fear of death and will never again be controlled or tortured by your mind. False ideas and beliefs will dissolve. In their place will be clarity, happiness, joy, peace, infinite fun and wonder—every moment a delight. You will know you are safe and secure no matter what.

"And when we recognize this . . . ultimate happiness is established permanently, and forever. And with its establishment comes immortality, unlimitedness, imperturbable peace, total freedom, and everything else that everyone is seeking."
Lester Levenson, from Happiness Is Free, *volumes 1–5*

When you fully recognize who you are, life becomes effortless—everything you need seems to appear without any effort from you. There's an ease and a flow that take over your life. A life of lack and limitation is over forever. You come to know the ultimate power you have over everything in the world.

When you fully recognize who you are, suffering and struggle will be gone, and fear and negative emotions will dissolve. The mind will quiet. You will be filled with joy, positivity, fulfillment, a sense of abundance, and an imperturbable peace. This will be your life.

From the words of Jan Frazier, a mother and literary teacher:

"Imagine this: Whatever has weighed on you suddenly no longer weighs. It may still be there, a fact in your life, but it has no mass, no gravity. All that has ever troubled you is now just a feature of the landscape, like a tree, a passing cloud. Every bit of emotional and mental turmoil has ceased: the entire burden, some form of which has been with you as long as you can remember. A thing familiar as your closest friend—as much a part of you as the language you speak, the color of your skin—is utterly, inexplicably gone. Into the startling emptiness flows a quiet joy that buoys you morning, noon, and night, that goes everywhere you go, into any kind of circumstance, even into sleep. Everything you undertake happens effortlessly. You are happy, but for no reason. Nothing bothers you. You feel no stress. When a problem arises, you know what to do, you do it, and then you let it go. People that used to drive you crazy no longer do. While you feel compassion for others' suffering, you don't suffer yourself. Activities that used to be tedious are fun. You don't need therapy; you don't get bored, anxious, or moody. Except when needed for a task, your mind is at rest. Your life is entirely fulfilled—without your having to do anything to fulfill it, . . . you know that no matter what challenge you are handed—for the rest of your life—the peace will sustain. Never again will you be afraid, desperate, lonely. Whatever comes your way, this causeless joy will hold. Imagine it."

Jan Frazier, from When Fear Falls Away

This is your life with The Greatest Secret. This is your destiny.

CHAPTER 1 *Summary*

- *Whether we realize it or not, we've been in search of The Greatest Secret unceasingly every single day of our lives.*

- *This great secret is in plain view for every one of us to see, yet we've missed it.*

- *We've missed the truth for thousands of years because we are distracted by our problems, the drama in our lives, the comings and goings of the events in the world.*

- *We've accepted many false ideas and beliefs throughout our lives, and they have kept us enslaved.*

- *Whenever we suffer, it's because we've mistaken our own identity.*

- *Humanity is suffering from a misunderstanding of our true nature.*

- *You are having the* experience *of being a person, but in the bigger picture it's not who you are.*

- *You're supposed to be happy all the time. Happiness is your true nature.*

- *Discovering who you really are has been given many names: enlightenment, self-realization, self-discovery, awakening, remembering.*

- *Open yourself to the possibility that you can experience* the truth *of what you are, this very moment.*

- *When you fully recognize who you are, you will experience a life without problems, upset, hurt, worry, or fear, and you will be filled with joy, positivity, fulfillment, abundance, and peace.*

The Greatest Secret: Revealed

"So close you can't see it.
So subtle your mind can't understand it.
So simple you can't believe it.
So good you can't accept it."
Loch Kelly, from Shift into Freedom *regarding the Shangpa Kagyu Tibetan Buddhist tradition*

Why is it so few have discovered the truth? Why haven't the majority of us realized who we are? How can billions of people have missed something so vitally important to our happiness?

We've missed discovering The Greatest Secret because of one small obstacle: a belief! Just a single belief has prevented us from making the greatest discovery we can make. That belief is that we are our body and our mind.

You Are Not Your Body

"We came into this world to be a body in order to learn that we are not a body."
Lester Levenson, from Happiness Is Free, *volumes 1–5*

Just as you use a car to get from one location to another, your body is a vehicle you use to move around and to experience the world.

"If you have a car, you do not say you are the car. Why then, if you have a body, do you say you are the body?"
Lester Levenson, from Happiness Is Free, *volumes 1–5*

Being material, your body isn't conscious. It doesn't know it's a body, but "you" know it's a body. Your toe doesn't know it's a toe, your wrist doesn't know it's a wrist, your head doesn't know it's a head, and your brain has no idea it's a brain, but "you" know each and every part of your body. How could you be the body when you know all the different parts, and yet not one of them knows you?

It's probing questions like these that enabled the great beings of the past to unravel the mystery behind who we really are.

"The worst habit we have gotten into over the millenniums is that we believe we are this body."
Lester Levenson, from Happiness Is Free, *volumes 1–5*

"We have forgotten what we are, and we have identified ourselves with objects. I am this body, therefore I'm going to die."
Francis Lucille

"You fear that if the body isn't, you are not."
Lester Levenson

Believing you're just your body creates the biggest fear of humanity, the fear of death: when your body dies, you fear you will no longer exist. It's like a dark cloud hanging over your life.

"If you want immortality—stop holding on to the body."
Lester Levenson, from Happiness Is Free, *volumes 1–5*

It's good news that you're not your body, because your body is going to come to an end one day, as all material things do. The world is completely made up of material things, and not one of those things will last, including your body, which appears and disappears through the process of birth and death. What you *actually* are never dies!

"What you truly are cannot die. The body will die, but the body is not what you are."
Mooji

"We have free will to identify with the body or identify with who we really are. Body equals pain and what you are equals infinite joy."
Lester Levenson, from Happiness Is Free, *volumes 1–5*

Your way out of all difficulties begins with letting go of the belief that you are your body.

You Are Not Your Mind

The voice in your head is not you, yet you've probably believed it is you for most of your life. While the voice in your head sounds like you, seems to know a lot about you, and has become very familiar to you, it's definitely *not* you. That voice in your head is your mind, and you are not your mind.

"The mind is a collection of thoughts that constantly appear and disappear."
Peter Lawry

"If there are no thoughts, then there is no mind. Mind is only thought."
Lester Levenson, from Happiness Is Free, *volumes 1–5*

Check for yourself. Where is your mind if there is no thought? Your mind isn't there.

"There's nothing inside but thoughts and feelings, memories and sensations, but are you a thought? Are you a feeling?"
Rupert Spira, from a public talk

If you were a thought—let's say, a frustrated thought—then you would disappear when the frustrated thought disappeared. You are not a thought, a sensation, or a feeling, because when they end you would end too, but you're still here after they end. You are here before a thought, you are here before a feeling or sensation, and you remain perfectly intact after they've gone. It's fairly obvious when you look at it. Certainly, we do experience thoughts, feelings, and sensations, but we are none of those things.

In some ways it's easy to understand how we've missed seeing who we really are, because the body and mind are a very convincing combination. Our mind keeps up a constant tirade of thoughts, most of which include the word "I," as though the mind is us. And you may be surprised to learn that all our bodily sensations come from the mind, too, which reinforces our belief that we are our body.

"How others see you contributes to your sense of self. When things happen, they seem to happen 'to' you, or you may bring them about . . . You care what happens because of its effect on you. You 'hold' yourself with a wish to keep yourself safe and in a good light. You certainly do seem real."

Jan Frazier, from The Great Sweetening: Life After Thought

It's not that you don't have a body and a mind; it's just that they are not the *real* you. Just like your car, they're simply finely tuned instruments you're using to experience the material world.

"Identifying with the body and mind is the only thing that is covering up who you truly are. It's this misidentification that is veiling your true Self."

Mooji

Are You Really the Person You Think You Are?

"Considering all the effort given to bolstering the ego—the emphasis on self-esteem, reputation, achievement, physical appearance, material acquisition—it's a miracle awakening ever happens at all."

Jan Frazier, from The Freedom of Being

The ego, the imagined self, the pretend self, the separate self, and the psychological self are a few of the names that teachers and sages have given for our mistaken identity. All of these descriptions refer to a body and a mind that together make up what we call a person. When we refer to ourselves, most of us are referring to this person that we think we are.

"A person is what you experience, it is not what you are."
Mooji

"There's no such thing as a person. If you say, 'I'm a person,' then you have to say which one—there was a baby once upon a time, there was a teenager, there was a toddler . . . and then this whole process will be over soon."
Deepak Chopra™, M.D.

Your personality is constantly changing, so if your personality is you, which person are you? Are you the angry person, the loving person, the frustrated person, the irritated person, or the kind person? You probably think you're all of them, but you can't be all of them because if you were, the angry person would never disappear; it would always be here. Or if the frustrated person were really you, when the frustrated person disappeared, a bit of you would disappear with it. But that doesn't happen, does it? You're here before the angry person appears, and you're here after the angry person disappears. You're here before the frustrated person appears, and you're here after they disappear. Clearly you are not your changing moods or personality.

"Personality is a useful tool, but it cannot define who you are. Who you are lies far beyond who you think you are."
Jac O'Keeffe

"The biggest obstacle to discovering the truth of who we essentially are is the belief that I am a cluster of thoughts, memories, feelings and sensations. Together these form an illusory self or entity. The

belief that I am this entity is the only obstacle. All our psychological problems are due to this imaginary self. It always comes down to mistaking ourselves for this."
Rupert Spira, from a public talk

"The person only seems to exist because of the persistent and unquestioned belief that there is an actual 'person' here. But the person, or ego, can't exist without the belief in it. It's only imagination. In truth, there's no person at all. The only resident of this house of the body is the pure Self, which is what you are. The rest is all made up. There are not two tenants in this body, there's only ever been one. Belief in ego gives a sense of reality, but this is not a fact, only a fiction."
Mooji

What's the problem with believing we're an ego or a person?

We feel small and extremely vulnerable. We're afraid of bad things happening to us. We're afraid of illness, getting old, and dying. We're afraid of losing the things we have, and not getting the things we want. We live in a state of lack, believing there's "not enough": not enough money, not enough time, not enough energy, not enough love, health, or happiness, and not enough life. And even worse, we believe *we're* not enough. None of this is true—in fact, it is the very opposite of the truth—but we can never have true lasting happiness while we hold on to the belief that we're only a person.

"The tragedy and comedy of the human condition is that we spend most of our lives thinking, feeling, acting, perceiving and relating on behalf of an illusory self."
Rupert Spira, from The Ashes of Love

"The ego isn't who you are. But it makes so much racket you can't hear who you really are. If you keep it going, if you feed and water the ego, it's madness."
Jan Frazier, from Opening the Door

"I think everyone is suffering from person poison . . . living life too personally, perceiving life too personally, taking things too personally. When you're responding to life in a personal mode it is a form of blindness. You don't see things in their correct light."
Mooji

You are most certainly *experiencing* a body, *experiencing* a mind, and having the *experience* of being a person, but these are actually the least parts of you, and ultimately they are not you, because when they end, *you* do not end.

"There is 'no people' in people."
Shakti Caterina Maggi

But there is a *real* you.

"Why is it so hard to see through the ego, to let it go—to stop believing in the solidity of the little guy? Why do we hold on to this apparently real self, when beneath and around and above and swimming all through it is this gorgeous other reality that really is real, that can be counted on for sustenance, for perfect peacefulness? Why deny ourselves this, for the sake of something so paltry by comparison—for a thing that causes so much trouble, even pain?"
Jan Frazier, from Opening the Door

Big Pretenders

Your thoughts, feelings, sensations, and beliefs seamlessly work together to convince you you're a person. We're all big pretenders. We're pretending we're very small. We're pretending we're very limited. We're pretending we're a small, limited person who is born, lives for a time, dies, and that's the end of us. But nothing could be further from the truth!

"We are self-obsessed with an imaginary character that doesn't exist."
Shakti Caterina Maggi

We could say that this imaginary character is exactly like a movie character. We know the actor playing the character exists, but does the movie character know that the actor exists? No, the movie character is imaginary.

We cement our belief that we're a person with every thought. If you check on any thought, you'll find that there's a "me" at the center of every one of them. Those thoughts centered around the "me" you believe yourself to be affirm over and over again that you're a little, limited person.

When you believe the voice in your head is who you are, you automatically believe everything it says; you believe all the thoughts that your mind generates.

Thoughts like:
"I'm getting old."
"I'm too tired."
"I'm not good enough."
"I can't do it."
"I don't have enough time."
"I'm not as healthy as I used to be."
"I don't have enough money."
"I'm not smart enough."
"My eyesight is not as good as it used to be."
"I don't feel loved."
"He or she doesn't approve of me."
"I don't deserve it."
"I'm scared of dying."
"I don't know what to do."

These thoughts are all limitations, imposed on you by your mind. Who you really are is *un*limited, which means absolutely nothing has power over you!

My teacher says that we're practicing being small through constant limited thoughts (like the ones I just listed), and if we were not practicing being a small, limited person, we would see the truth of who we really are.

Everything about a "person" is the very opposite of who you really are. The person is imperfect. The real you is perfect. The person is temporary and limited. The real you is permanent and unlimited. The person is born and dies. The real you is never born and never dies. The person is personal and unstable. The real you is impersonal and always stable. The person has changing moods. The real you is constant happiness and peace. The person is full of judgments and opinions. The real you is allowing and accepting of everything. The person gets sick and becomes old. The real you is not subject to aging, and sickness can never touch you. The person suffers. The real you is free of all pain and suffering. The person dies. The real you exists for all eternity.

Trading Unhappiness for Truth

There's only one way to have a blissful life with lasting happiness, and that is to know your true nature. There's only one way out of a life plagued with problems, negativity, and discord, and that is to know the truth of who you really are.

"The real you is infinitely grand and glorious, whole, perfect, and in total peace, and you are blinding yourself to this by assuming that you are a limited ego. Drop the blinder, the ego, and be forever in perfect peace and joy. When you have found yourself—you will have everything."

Lester Levenson, from Happiness Is Free, *volumes 1–5*

"Life is not about solving lots of little problems because they will never end. Life points us to the one essential thing that has been overlooked—our own true and unchanging self. Mankind as a whole is living largely in the mistaken *idea* that we are fundamentally a person with a body as opposed to our true Self."
Mooji

"There may be tragedy in the 'story' of our lives, but in truth, there is no tragedy happening to us. Ultimately, the story is only there to teach us this distinction. The moment we take the lesson even the story changes to reveal itself as beauty, love, and intelligence. Do not be attached to the concept that misery is unavoidable. As long as we are attached to this concept, there will be misery."
Francis Lucille

"In the biblical parable, the man who is identified with the body/mind is the man who built his house on sand. To realize one's true nature is to build one's house on rock."
David Bingham

There's no search to find the truth because it is what you already are. How could you search for yourself? It's only that the majority of us have been constantly looking away from our true selves, rather than looking at who we are.

Have you ever looked at one of those pictures where there are two images in the one picture? When you first look at the picture, you can see one image clearly, but at first you can't see the second image. You try, but the second image seems to elude you due to your focus on the first image.

You have to change your perspective and soften your gaze *ever so slightly* to see the other image come into view.

In Rubin's famous picture, at first either you see two people looking at each other, or you see a vase. To see both images clearly you have to shift the way you're looking at the picture.

For most of our lives we've been looking at ourselves from the perspective that we are a body and mind—that we are a person. But to see clearly who we are, just as for Rubin's painting, we have to shift our perspective—ever so slightly.

The Reveal

Let me ask you one simple question.

Are you aware?

Your answer must be "yes," otherwise you wouldn't be aware of the question I just asked you. Let me ask you again.

Are you aware?

Yes, you're aware. You were aware as a baby, through your childhood, your teenage years, and throughout adulthood. You've been aware your entire life.

Awareness is and has been the only constant in your life. Your body keeps changing, your mind keeps changing, thoughts, feelings, and sensations all keep changing, but the one thing that has never changed is your awareness of it all.

And that awareness *is who you really are*.

You are Awareness.

"You are it. It's so close you cannot see it. You look through its eyes at the world around you."
Jan Frazier, from The Freedom of Being

"When we say 'I,' we've been conditioned to believe that we're referring to the body, when really 'I' is referring to Awareness."
David Bingham

You are not a body, a mind, or a bundle of thoughts, feelings, memories, or sensations. You are the one who is *aware* of your body, your mind, your thoughts, feelings, memories, and sensations. You are Awareness itself.

"The moment you meet Awareness something in you recognizes it."
Mooji

You're aware of reading this book. You're aware of the sounds around you. You're aware of the room you're in. You're aware of your name. You're aware of your body and the clothes on your body, your breathing, and bodily sensations. You're aware of the roof of your mouth, the soles of your feet, and your fingers. You're aware of your mind, the thoughts in your head, and your feelings and moods.

In fact, you couldn't know or experience any of life at all without Awareness.

You Are The Awareness That Is Aware of Everything

Awareness is what is aware of every single life experience you have. It's not the mind or the body that is aware of your life. You—the Awareness that you are—are aware of the mind, thoughts, and the body, and anything you are aware of cannot be you.

The teacher Sailor Bob Adamson points out that we know we exist— of that we have no doubt. Well, the only way we know that we exist is our awareness that we exist. We make the mistake of believing our awareness that we exist comes from the mind or the body, but that is not true. Our awareness that we exist is what we truly are, not the mind or the body.

Just for a moment, imagine you have no body or mind.

Take away your body.

Take away your mind.

Take away your name.

Take away your life story, which is your entire past.

Take away all memory, beliefs, and all thought.

And notice what is left.

What is left is simply Awareness.

"If someone were to draw our attention to the white paper on which these words are written, we would suddenly become aware of it. In fact, we were always aware of the paper but we didn't realise it due to the exclusive focus of our attention on the words. Awareness is like the white paper."
Rupert Spira, from Being Aware of Being Aware

Just like the white paper, Awareness is always present in the background of our life. We usually give our exclusive attention to our mind and thoughts and our body and sensations, because they're very attention grabbing. But we could not experience the mind and its thoughts or the body and its sensations without Awareness to be aware of them, just as we could not see any words if it were not for the background of the paper the words were printed on.

"Give your attention to this background, even a little, and you will discover a whole new world."
Hale Dwoskin

"Awareness is the most obvious element of experience and yet the most overlooked."
Rupert Spira, from Being Aware of Being Aware

"The subtle thing that is overlooked is that everything is known directly by awareness, but it's assumed that everything is coming in through the mind. For instance, the common thing would be to say, 'I think,' but actually, if it's looked at carefully, it's noticed that there is an awareness of thinking . . . so the thinking isn't who you are; there's something that is aware of thinking."
David Bingham, from Conscious TV

The one that is looking out through your eyes is Awareness! The one that is hearing through your ears is Awareness! Without Awareness you wouldn't be aware of anything you see, hear, taste, smell, or touch, and you would have no experience of the information coming in through your senses. Your senses aren't aware; it's Awareness that's aware of all of your senses.

"The apparatus with which we see is by itself inert, unable to see. A telescope is useless without an astronomer behind it. It doesn't see anything by itself. Likewise, the apparatus of mind doesn't see anything by itself."
Francis Lucille, from The Perfume of Silence

"You are the Awareness that is aware of everything."
David Bingham

"This individual consciousness—our feeling 'I am a person, a separate individual, a mind or soul confined within the limits of a body'—is merely an imagination, a false and distorted form of our pure consciousness 'I am,' but it is nevertheless the root cause of all desire and all misery."
Michael James, from Happiness and the Art of Being

"The 'me' that we imagine we are is just another thought."
Kalyani Lawry

"Our real nature, the infinite real self that we are, is simply us minus the mind."
Lester Levenson, from Happiness Is Free, *volumes 1–5*

Our mind distorts the world we see by layering veils of thought and belief, one over the top of each other. Each mental veil distorts the world further and prevents us from seeing everything the way it really is.

"The mind will never discover who you are because the mind is the cover-up of who you are. It's only by letting go of the mind that you will discover who you are."
Lester Levenson, from Happiness Is Free, *volumes 1–5*

Trying to see the truth with your mind is like trying to see something with a blindfold on. You need to drop the blindfold to see, just as you need to drop the mind to see who you really are.

"Attempting to understand consciousness with your mind is like trying to illuminate the sun with a candle."
Mooji, from White Fire, *second edition*

Without even realizing it, most of us are constantly focused on the noise of thoughts coming from our mind. Awareness is always present, but when there's a break from the noise of thoughts, it's much easier to notice it. When thoughts stop, we become consciously aware of Awareness, which has been existing silently in the background all along.

The Mind's Cover-Up

"We're so used to knowing ourselves through our troubles, our dramas, and our obsessions that awake awareness, which is our true nature and our basic goodness, is hard to accept as our true identity."
Loch Kelly, from Shift into Freedom

"Awake Awareness" is the name that Loch Kelly uses for Awareness, and it is just one of the many different names used by teachers past and present to describe what you are: Awareness, Awake Awareness, Consciousness, Cosmic Consciousness, Being, Buddha Nature, Christ Consciousness, God Consciousness, Spirit, the Self, Infinite Being, Infinite Intelligence, Unlimited Being, True Nature, True Self, Presence of God, Presence, Presence Awareness, Pure Consciousness, Pure Awareness, and many others. All these words are describing exactly the same thing—the Awareness that you are.

"We're so smart and our lives are so complex that it's hard to believe that simply discovering awake awareness could be the solution to our suffering. It's also hard to believe that the most important discovery is already here within us; we don't have to go on an odyssey to find it, earn it, or develop it."
Loch Kelly, from Shift into Freedom

"The great joke is the simplicity of it all."
Peter Lawry

It's a great joke because what we truly are, what is closer to us than our very breath, has eluded the majority of humans for thousands of years.

We've missed the simplest, most wonderful discovery because our thoughts have a hypnotic effect on us that keeps us in our head, oblivious to Awareness. We usually give our attention exclusively to the thoughts in our mind and to everything we perceive through our senses, and with our attention diverted we miss what is always present—Awareness.

"There is nothing wrong with the body or the mind. The only problem is that we identify our witnessing presence, consciousness, with them. As long as we identify this witnessing presence with the body and the mind, there is no room for this presence to reveal itself in all its glory."
Francis Lucille, from The Perfume of Silence

"For a moment, take off the persona. It's just an item of clothing, threadbare, stained with years of wear and tear."
Pamela Wilson

"To believe that our Self—luminous, open, empty Awareness— shares the limits and the destiny of the mind and body is like believing that the screen shares the limits and destiny of a character in a movie."
Rupert Spira, from The Ashes of Love

"People think they are a human being, but they're the Infinite Being. They've mistaken their identity, but who they really are has never left them and is always present."
David Bingham

Your mind appears only when you have a thought, and it disappears after the thought has ended. But Awareness never appears and disappears. Awareness is always present, even when you're asleep. It *feels* like Awareness disappears when you go to sleep and appears again when you wake, and yet you know when you've had a great night's sleep because you say something like, "I slept really well. I slept like a baby." How do you know that you slept like a baby? You know it because Awareness was aware and present the entire time you were sleeping.

When you ask yourself the question, "Am I aware?" immediately Awareness is noticed. It didn't appear; it was always present. You simply took your attention from *thinking* and put it on *Awareness*, and so you became consciously aware.

Everything other than Awareness eventually ends or dies. Without exception, all material earthly things come and go, appear and disappear. Every single thing on earth—bodies, cities, countries, oceans—appears and eventually disappears. Take a moment to think about it, and you'll see that nothing remains. It's all temporary, even planet earth itself, the sun, the solar system, even universes. Nothing is here forever, except for one thing—Awareness. You, Awareness, are here forever!

Our bodies age, yet when people get older they'll say they don't feel they've aged, and that they feel the same as they always have. They'll admit that their body feels older, but the one they feel themselves to be deep down doesn't feel like it has aged at all. Without realizing it, they are sensing the timeless Awareness that they really are.

"When you remember your past, your childhood, who is it that remembers? I remember. 'I' is that which knows the experience, remembers the experience."
Deepak Chopra™, M.D.

The "I" that we call ourselves at five years old, fifteen years old, thirty years old, and sixty years old is the ageless Awareness that has witnessed our entire life.

Five years old: "I . . . am going to school soon."

Fifteen years old: "I . . . can't wait to graduate."

Thirty years old: "I . . . just got engaged."

Sixty years old: "I . . . am not ready for retirement yet."

"Self-realization is to see that the changing appearances on the surface of life are arising within the permanent, ever-stable Awareness that one truly is and has only ever been."
David Bingham, from Conscious TV

"This is not a fairy tale. This possible thing is as real as a tree, as real as politics, as the roots that hold the tree to the ground, as real as the newspaper and its stories. It is as real as the Red Sox, as the price of gas, as a fight with your in-laws, as real as a tuition bill . . . The truth is, it is more real than these things, and yet it is hardly seen, hardly felt, let alone directly known."
Jan Frazier, from Opening the Door

"There is not one of us who is not in direct touch with, in possession of, an infinite Beingness that's all perfect, all present, all joyous and eternal. There is not one of us who is not in direct contact with That right now! But due to wrong learning, by assuming, over the ages, concepts of limitation and by looking outwardly, we have beclouded the view. We have covered over this Infinite Being that we are with concepts of, 'I am this physical body,' or, 'I am this mind,' or, 'With this physical body and mind, I have heaps and heaps of problems and troubles.'"

Lester Levenson, from Happiness Is Free, *volumes 1–5*

"This is the same state that most religions refer to as 'liberation' or 'salvation,' because only in this state of true self-knowledge are we free or saved from the bondage of mistaking ourself to be a separate individual, a consciousness that is confined within the limits of a physical body."

Michael James, from Happiness and the Art of Being

Consciousness or Awareness is also known by some religions as the presence of God. When a person has a divine experience—an experience where they feel they were touched by God—the individual mind and ego drop, which then reveals Awareness, or the presence of God. There is a feeling of pure love, infinite peace, beauty, happiness, and bliss, which cannot be mistaken for anything but divinity.

"In reality, we are the Infinite Being rather than the human being. We are the Infinite Being, having a human experience."

David Bingham

In many ways, the truth of life and of ourselves is actually the complete opposite to what we have been taught. Instead of looking outward to the world for happiness, for fulfillment, for answers and truth, we need to turn and look inward, because it's only in that direction that we will find everything we're looking for. Our breathtaking world, and everything in it, is meant to be enjoyed to the fullest, but the happiness, joy, love, peace, intelligence, and freedom that are Awareness—your very nature—can only be found within you.

CHAPTER 2 *Summary*

- A single belief has prevented us from making the greatest discovery—the belief that we are our body and our mind.

- You are not your body; your body is a vehicle you use to experience the world. Your body isn't conscious.

- Believing you're your body creates the biggest fear of humanity, the fear of death.

- What you actually are never dies.

- You are not your mind; mind is only thoughts. If there are no thoughts, then there is no mind.

- You are not a thought, a sensation, or a feeling, because if you were, when they end you would end too.

- Your body and mind together make up what we call a person—the imagined self.

- A person is what you experience, it is not what you are.

- We can never have true lasting happiness while we hold on to the belief that we're a person.

- You are experiencing a body, experiencing a mind, and having the experience of being a person, but they are not you.

- *We're pretending we're a small, limited person through constant thoughts of limitation.*

- *Who you really are is* unlimited, *which means absolutely nothing has power over you.*

- *You've been aware your entire life; Awareness is and has been the only constant in your life.*

- *That awareness is who you* really *are.* You are awareness.

- *You couldn't know or experience any of life without awareness.*

- *It's not the mind or the body that is aware of your life. Awareness is what is aware of every single life experience you have.*

- *Imagine you have no body or mind, name, life story, past, memory, beliefs, or thought. What is left is Awareness.*

- *We usually give our attention exclusively to thoughts and to everything we perceive, so we miss what is always present—Awareness.*

- *Awareness is present even when you're asleep.*

- *When you ask yourself the question, "Am I aware?" immediately awareness is noticed. It didn't appear; it was always present.*

- *Everything other than awareness eventually ends or dies.*

- *The "I" that we call ourselves at every age is the ageless "I" of Awareness, which has witnessed our entire life.*

- *Instead of looking outward to the world for happiness, we need to turn and look inward; it's only in that direction that we will find everything we're looking for.*

CHAPTER 3

THE REVEAL
CONTINUED

You *are* Awareness; you're not a person *being aware* of something. You are Infinite Awareness itself.

As Francis Lucille said, a telescope is just an instrument without the astronomer looking through it. Your body and mind are instruments too. And so what's looking through your eyes? You, Awareness! What's hearing sounds? You, Awareness! Your body is alive because of Awareness—Awareness is actually the life force that animates your body.

"The fundamental mistake is to believe a human being is experiencing awareness. This is not correct. Only awareness is aware, and therefore only awareness can experience awareness. When I ask you, 'Are you aware?,' you will pause to check your experience and you will answer, 'Yes.' That 'yes' is an affirmation of awareness's awareness of itself. It is not a body or a brain that experiences being aware. The body and brain are *experienced*; they don't experience."

Rupert Spira, from the talk "The Light of Consciousness"

There Is Only One: Our Name Is "I"

"Only awareness is aware. Human beings aren't aware. Dogs and cats aren't aware. Animals aren't aware. Only awareness is aware. There is only one awareness, just as there is only one space in the universe. That awareness is refracted in each of our minds and, as a result, each of our minds seems to have its own package of awareness, just as every building seems to contain its own space. But the awareness with which each of our minds is aware of its experience is the only awareness there is, infinite awareness, just as the space in all buildings is the same space."

Rupert Spira, from the talk "Awareness Is the Only Aware Entity in Existence"

This Infinite Awareness—this one and only Awareness—is *you*, and every other person! There is only one Awareness, and it's the same Awareness that is operating through everybody. There is just one of us. Our name is "I."

"There is only one 'I,' and you are It, as everyone is It."
David Bingham

It's the one Awareness operating through every living form. All the physical forms are simply different vehicles for the one glorious, Infinite Awareness. This is the true meaning of the teaching, "We are one."

Consciousness and Awareness are different words used to describe the same thing. They both describe you.

"This very ordinary consciousness, which is hearing these words right this moment, and understanding them, happens to be also the divine consciousness that lives all lives. There is not a single separate entity in the entire cosmos."
Francis Lucille, from Truth Love Beauty

"We are One. There is only one in us. There is only one as us."
Mooji, from White Fire, *second edition*

It's a little like the trillions of individual cells living, working, and operating in your body. Unbeknownst to each of the individual cells, they are really part of the one human being. There are billions of beings in the world, operating as individuals, and unbeknownst to most of them, they're the one and only Infinite Being.

"We have been taught to believe that this consciousness is personal and limited, and that each person is endowed with a private and separate consciousness, so that there are many consciousnesses. We have never considered that while it is easy to verify that two objects are separate, because it is possible to see their borders and limits, it is not possible to find any border or limit to consciousness."
Francis Lucille, from Truth Love Beauty

If there's only one Awareness or Consciousness, why aren't you aware of thoughts or sensations in other people's bodies? Or of what an animal in Africa is seeing or hearing? It's because Awareness or Consciousness has been funneled through your mind, making it localized to your body. Plus, the belief that you're a separate individual prevents you from experiencing the full expansiveness of Awareness. But when you feel compassion or love for another, you are far more tuned in to the one Awareness than you might have realized.

We've all had glimpses in our life of the Awareness that we are, but more often than not we passed them off as something we imagined or a trick of the mind. Whether we remember them or not, we've had experiences that we can't explain, very often when we were children. It may have been an experience where you felt you expanded to be really big, and felt like the world was within you, or maybe you saw or heard something that no one else could see or hear.

Children are more tuned in to Awareness because their mind hasn't yet covered Awareness over with a whole array of mental concepts and beliefs. Under the age of two and a half, children are pure, simple Awareness. They don't have the experience of being separate, which is why they refer to themselves in the third person. On seeing herself in a photograph, two-year-old Sarah will point and say, "That's Sarah!" She won't say, "That's me," because she's not yet *experiencing herself* as a "me," a separate person. Her experience is that there's only One and she is it, and everyone else is it.

"There's nothing out there but our consciousness. There's only one consciousness and we're it."
Lester Levenson, from Happiness Is Free, *volumes 1–5*

Awareness or Consciousness is all through your body and everywhere outside your body; Awareness can't be contained within your body because Awareness is formless. It would be like trying to contain space in a jar; of course, space is both inside the jar and everywhere outside the jar. In fact, the jar is *in space,* just as all bodies are *in Awareness.* Absolutely everything is contained in Awareness, and it's the reason why the enlightened beings' experience of life is that they are everything—because they *are* everything. And as Awareness, so are you!

"Behind your eyes is the same consciousness, the only consciousness that is behind Jesus, Buddha, Krishna, and behind all eyes."
My teacher

Think about that. Your Consciousness is the same Consciousness as all of the great beings; that's how close you are to them. They are not at a distance from you. You are *one* with them.

"The mystery, the magic of it is that this ordinary consciousness that we take for granted, even as far as denying its existence, happens to be the consciousness of the universe itself, its true center."
Francis Lucille, from Truth Love Beauty

How To Stay as Awareness

There's no process to become the Awareness that you are; it's not something you have to attain. This is not something that certain people have and you don't have. You *are already it*, right now. You may have overlooked it, and you may have believed all your life that you were just a person, but that doesn't alter the fact of what you actually are.

"You can lose everything else, but you can never lose the awareness that you are."
Mooji, from Vaster Than Sky, Greater Than Space

When a human being lives from the place of knowing they're Infinite Awareness, then the experience of living in the material world becomes breathtaking. Because their mind has dropped to the background and Awareness is in the foreground, they are no longer subject to the turmoil of the mind, so they are lighthearted, happy all the time, and laugh a lot. They're existing in pure happiness and bliss and living their lives from that place every day. Problems are virtually nonexistent, everything dreamed of comes to them, and because they're consciously living as Awareness, they're fully aware of their immortality. They know they are everything, and yet they know they're not affected by anything. Life on earth doesn't get any better than this!

"Every little thing you do or see—every little, ordinary thing— carries this tingly sense of being. It is hard not to cry sometimes at the most unspectacular things. The lines of the walls in relation to the flat of the floor. Its horizontality. The nap of the rug. The sound of the car going by. The smell of the skin on your arm. All is miraculous."

Jan Frazier, from Opening the Door

But you have to experience it for yourself. Hearing it from someone else is a guide, pointing you in the right direction. It's like a travel agent describing Mount Everest. You can't know what Mount Everest is like until you get there and experience it for yourself—only then will you know.

"It is actually impossible not to remain as this open space of consciousness. However, to be it knowingly is a different matter."
Francis Lucille, from The Perfume of Silence

"You cannot be out of awareness—it is missed simply through the habit of placing the attention in the thinking."
Peter Lawry

We can put our attention either on the thoughts in our head or on the Awareness that we are. It's a simple shift of your attention. Put your attention on Awareness as often as you can rather than giving your attention to thinking, and you will be on your way to absolute freedom and bliss.

The Awareness Practice
Three Steps to Bliss

The Awareness Practice is what I use and continue to practice to consciously stay as Awareness. This practice is not to *become* Awareness, because you're that already. It's so you can live your life consciously as the Awareness that you are. It's just three simple steps to a life of total freedom and lasting, blissful happiness.

Step 1. Ask yourself, "Am I aware?"
Step 2. Notice Awareness.
Step 3. Stay as Awareness.

Step 1. Ask Yourself, "Am I Aware?"

Don't try to answer the question with your mind; thoughts cannot help you experience Awareness. Each time you ask the question, your attention will be taken away from thinking and the mind and put on Awareness. When you ask, "Am I aware?" Awareness is present instantly. The mind may come in quickly afterward with a thought, but if it does, simply ask the question again. The more you ask the question, the longer you will remain as Awareness, and the quieter your thoughts and your mind will become.

"Notice that the mind, in all its changes, has a changeless background."
Hale Dwoskin

After asking, "Am I aware?" the first thing you'll likely feel is a sense of relief as any resistance you are holding in the mind and body starts to melt away. After repeatedly asking the question, over time the feeling of relief will turn into a subtle feeling of peaceful happiness. You may feel a sense of serenity, as your mind becomes quiet. You may feel currents of joy running through the area around your heart.

The relief you feel is due to your mind falling into the background. The longer the mind remains in the background, with Awareness present in the foreground, the greater the relief, and the more happiness you will begin to feel. Bliss comes when Awareness remains permanently in the foreground, and the mind is delegated to its rightful place.

Remember, Awareness is formless, so it's not something you can hold on to. It's like love. You know love exists, but can you hold on to it? You can feel the sensations of love in your heart, but you can't grasp it in your hand. It's the same with Awareness. You will feel the sensations of relief and happiness in your body from Awareness, but you can't grasp it or hold on to it.

It can seem difficult to consciously stay as Awareness in the beginning, because of the habit of thinking.

"As soon as this is noticed, we may ask again, 'Am I Aware?,' in this way inviting the mind away from the objects of knowledge or experience, towards its essence or source."
Rupert Spira, from Being Aware of Being Aware

The way to break the habit of incessant thinking is by being the Infinite Awareness that you are. You can't use the mind to stop the mind and break the habit of thinking. It's the reason many people fail at meditation, because they're trying to use the mind to quiet the mind, instead of allowing the thoughts to come and go without giving them any attention.

For most people there's virtually no relief from their mind because it's constantly throwing up one thought after another, and they don't realize they can remove their attention from their thoughts. Freedom from the mind is such a glorious relief, and it comes when you can observe thoughts rather than being lured into following them and believing them.

Step 2. Notice Awareness

In a relatively short time of practicing step 1, you'll get to the point where you automatically notice Awareness. You won't need to ask, "Am I aware?" anymore, because in the moment you think of Awareness, instantly Awareness will be in the foreground and your mind will recede into the background.

"Allow the experience of being aware to come into the foreground of experience, and let thoughts, images, feelings, sensations and perceptions recede into the background. Simply notice the experience of being aware. The peace and happiness for which all people long reside there."

Rupert Spira, from Being Aware of Being Aware

Shift your attention to Awareness by noticing Awareness multiple times throughout the day. It won't be long before you feel a sense of exquisite relief and happiness each time you return from the turmoil of the mind to the deep peace of Awareness.

"There's a fork in every moment. To be what you are or what you are not. You're choosing in every second."

My teacher

If you feel like your mind is covering Awareness, or you feel like you've lost it and you can't get it back, ask yourself, "What is aware that Awareness is lost?" It's Awareness that's aware of it! And with that, you will be aware of Awareness.

If you don't think you've been able to discover Awareness yet, ask yourself, "What is aware that I haven't discovered Awareness?" It's Awareness that's aware of that too! And now you're aware of Awareness.

"You are already awareness itself, not the one trying to be aware."
Mooji

Are you aware of your body right now? It's Awareness that's aware of your body. Are you aware of the seat you're sitting on? It's Awareness that's aware of the seat. Are you aware of your breathing? It's Awareness that's aware of your breathing. It's that simple.

"Whenever you think of it, bring yourself back to the awareness of now. Do it hundreds of times each day, because, remember, all of your power is in your awareness of your power."
From The Secret

Step 3. Stay as Awareness

"In the beginning you feel like a visitor to awareness, but as you keep discovering the realness of it, any sense of fear or separation melts away."
Mooji

Staying as Awareness is all about where you put your attention. My teacher suggests a simple way to think about this. Our mind operates in a similar way to the lens on a camera. The mind has an automatic zoom function, and it focuses our attention on things in detail, just as you would zoom in with a camera lens for a close-up. The majority of the time the mind is zoomed in and we are seeing the world through focused attention, which results in a very narrow and distorted perspective of the world. But when you want to take a photograph of a wide-open space, you zoom out and open the lens as wide as you can for a wide-angle shot. In the same way, if you open your attention wide so you're not focused on any detail anymore, Awareness is revealed. It's a simple way to stay as Awareness and let everything be just as it is.

To put this into practice, take a look around you right now, find something close up to focus on, and focus your attention on only that. You can use your hand if you want. Now open your attention so it's very wide, taking in as much as possible of your surroundings without focusing on anything in particular. Notice an immediate sense of relief and relaxation in the body. This happens because our mind is constantly focused, and it takes a lot of effort to maintain that focus. So, when you open your attention to be as wide and open as possible, our mind dissolves into the background and Awareness comes into the foreground. You feel a sense of relief because Awareness is *effortless*; it sees and knows everything without any need to focus.

"The one that you've mistaken yourself for that wants to make things happen has zero power. Yet it's saying, 'I need to take care of some things.' It's Awareness that takes care of everything."
My teacher

"The less you believe you are the doer the more you are an unstoppable force for good in the world."
Hale Dwoskin

I used to be a big doer. I prided myself on my doing capabilities, juggling multiple things at one time. It became my identity. I was the Queen of Doing! And so of course the Universe flowed an unending number of things for me to do, because of what I believed about myself.

But that has all changed because of continually letting go of what I believed myself to be, and staying as the Awareness that I am. I'm not only happier than I've ever been, but instead of doing, doing, doing all the time, things just seem to get taken care of naturally, without me doing them. If I do end up doing something, it's like I'm not even doing it it's so effortless. Life becomes miraculous!

Give five minutes a day, at the very least, to putting your attention on Awareness. You can do it when you first wake up, when you get into bed, or at any other time that suits you. If you are as dedicated as I am to having a miraculous life, you will give your attention to Awareness more often, but even five minutes a day will make an enormous difference to your life. It's that easy.

Remember, this is not a practice to become Awareness, because you are Infinite Awareness already. Rather it's a practice that stops you from identifying yourself with the mind and body, which is not who you are.

"To begin with it seems like an effort to keep returning to the welcoming presence, but at some point, it is so natural that it seems to require an effort to leave it. It feels like home."
Francis Lucille, from The Perfume of Silence

You will reach a point where you know with certainty that you are in the realm of divinity, or for those who prefer to use the word "God," in the presence of God. To be in the presence of God or the realm of divinity is to be beyond the mind.

"When you lose the eyes of ego you see with the eyes of God."
Mooji

After doing these steps for a while, you'll discover that Awareness automatically becomes more dominant and present within you, and your mind becomes much quieter. Other indications of how you are doing are: your life will become easier and more effortless, you'll feel more peaceful, things that used to bother you won't bother you anymore, you'll feel calmer, your emotions will be more stable, and you'll find you're not easily swept away with negative emotions. In fact, you will begin to feel a sense of happiness that you've not felt before. You'll become more acutely aware of your mind's propensity to complain, criticize, and focus on negativity. And you'll find you're not giving your mind power over you like you used to, because you've taken your attention away from your thoughts.

"Knowing that we are the perfect Self, that we are not this limited body and mind, all problems immediately resolve."
Lester Levenson, from Happiness Is Free, *volumes 1–5*

Awareness is greater than every single thing it's aware of. The person is limited, but Awareness is unlimited, which means *everything* is possible. Nothing can ever restrict you; nothing whatsoever has power over you!

"We seem to have the experience of a limited consciousness but when we investigate more closely, we see that it is impossible. That which is aware of limitations transcends limitations and is therefore beyond them."

Francis Lucille, from The Perfume of Silence

Nothing can disturb Awareness! No number of problems can disrupt you. Negativity can't touch you. Wars can't affect you. You as Awareness are always safe and well. You are untouchable, unharmable, imperishable. What would there be to threaten you? You contain everything. You are everything. To the best of your ability, begin to stay as the Awareness that you are by putting your attention on Awareness often, so you can live a wondrous life.

"Then you can no more be fooled by the apparent limitations of the world. You see them as a dream, as an appearance, because you know that your very own Beingness has no limits."

Lester Levenson, from Happiness Is Free, *volumes 1–5*

CHAPTER 3 *Summary*

- *You* are *Awareness; you're not a person* being aware *of something.*

- *A telescope is just an instrument without the astronomer looking through it, and your body and mind are instruments of Awareness.*

- *There is only one awareness, and it's the same awareness that is operating through everybody.*

- *You aren't aware of thoughts or sensations in another person's body because Awareness has been funneled through your mind, making it localized to your body.*

- *Awareness or consciousness is all through your body and everywhere outside your body.*

- *We can put our attention either on the thoughts in our head or on the Awareness that we are. Put your attention on Awareness as often as you can.*

- *The Awareness Practice*
  Step 1. Ask yourself, "Am I aware?"
  Step 2. Notice Awareness.
  Step 3. Stay as Awareness.

- *The way to break the mind's habit of nonstop thinking once and for all is to stay as the Awareness that you are.*

- *Shift your attention to Awareness by noticing Awareness multiple times throughout the day.*

- *A simple way to stay as Awareness: Open your attention wide like the lens on a camera so you're not focused on any detail anymore, and Awareness is revealed.*

- *To practice, find something close up to focus on, and focus your attention on only that. Now open your attention so it's very wide, taking in as much as possible of your surroundings without focusing on anything in particular.*

CHAPTER 4

YOU'RE DREAMING . . . IT'S TIME TO WAKE UP

According to many spiritual teachers and ancient traditions, our entire world, your life and everyone else's life, is nothing more than a dream. They don't say that our world and everything in it is *like* a dream, but that it is literally made from the same substance as our dreams and is equally as illusory. When you are permanently staying as Awareness, you will know for certain that your life and the world are not the reality you thought they were: they are a dream.

"This life is a dream; we're dreaming we're a person living in a world that we are convinced is real. We don't realize it's all a dream. The whole world as now seen is nothing but a dream-illusion that never was. The truth is just behind the outward world."
Lester Levenson, from Happiness Is Free, *volumes 1–5*

"We should be open to the possibility that this is a dream and when we do, everything changes dramatically. It actually turns out to be so. If this waking experience is seen to be a dream, then our behavior changes and we will find that the response coming from the characters or the situation in this dream also changes."
Francis Lucille, from The Perfume of Silence

"We are right now in a lucid dream. And part of the dream is that which we call mind, body, and universe."
Deepak Chopra™, *M.D.*

"And the dream is seamless so it's virtually impossible for people to wake up."
My teacher

In your night dreams your mind creates your body, other people (some you know, some you don't know), cities, towns, houses, vehicles, food, objects, trees, nature, animals, the sun, stars, and sky. It also creates time passing, daytime, nighttime, voices, sounds, and every circumstance and event that takes place in your dream. Your mind creates an entire world, it creates a dream version of you, and it makes everything seem so real that you don't even question it—until you wake up! Only then do you realize it was a dream.

"You probably have noticed one of the main things about a dream. Virtually always, the "you" in the dream doesn't realize it's a dream. That's the ironic thing about dreaming. The characters in a dream automatically assume they are wide awake! The dream characters are not awake. The dream experiences are not real. But in the dream, none of that has been noticed. Notice something else about a dream. As far as the dream characters are concerned, there is nothing beyond the dream. The dream characters have no idea that there is another, real kind of awakeness. A dream character has no idea of what it's missing."
Peter Dziuban, from Simply Notice

"While we are subjected to the night dream, everything seems to be real. If we see a tiger, we are afraid because we don't know that we are creating the tiger. If we knew that we couldn't possibly be afraid, could we? This demonstrates that an illusion can seem to be quite real while we are subjected to it, even though, when we become aware of its illusory nature, we understand that it was we who were creating it all along."

Francis Lucille, from Truth Love Beauty

Even if you're fully aware that the world is a dream, you still remain respectful of its physicality, and of your physical body. You don't go and jump off a building, because the building, the ground, your body, and gravity are all made of the same dream stuff, and you will feel it! As one teacher said, if you come up and pinch me in a dream, I will feel it, because it's a dream pinch!

"In a dream, ten years may pass by in one minute. You may have a baby and then be taking it, as a child, to school. When you wake up,

you see that the body in the dream was an illusion, and the time to which it was subjected was also an illusion, but from the vantage point of the dream, it seemed to be real."
Francis Lucille, from The Perfume of Silence

"If we take the dream state as an example, there may be a dream that covers a fifty-year period, but we wake up and realize that it didn't actually happen. It only seemed real while there was identification with the dream state of consciousness. The waking state is also only an extremely convincing play that consciousness is producing."
David Bingham, from Conscious TV

"The laws of physics are the laws that apply to this waking dream. During night dreams, the laws of physics are different. That is why you can fly at night!"
Francis Lucille, from The Perfume of Silence

No matter what takes place in the "earth" dream, the end is the same for all of us: we wake up to discover that it was all a dream! This is why we're told by spiritual teachers to "wake up." It means waking up from the illusion and realizing that it's all a dream. When we wake up to the truth, we discover that no one was ever hurt or harmed, and no one died; just like when you wake up terrorized following a nightmare, and you realize with relief that no one was actually hurt and nothing bad happened, it was just a dream.

"If you can go to a movie and see a picture of war and suffering, and afterward say 'What a wonderful picture!' so may you take this life as a cosmic picture-show. Be prepared for every kind of experience that may come to you, realizing that all are but dreams."
Paramahansa Yogananda, from Man's Eternal Quest

"Seeing the world as a dream is a great practice, and it will help break its apparent solidity."
Francis Lucille

Waking Up

"The greatest healing is to wake up from what we are not."
Mooji

"It's like shifting your eyes from one thing to a different thing. It's that subtle. It's like exhaling. When you're ready, you'll do it. Don't tell yourself you'll never be ready. Don't tell yourself it's not possible. It's happening all around you, to people just like you. They aren't troubled anymore. They used to be. They are still living their lives. They are brimming in joy. They live lives of ease, no matter what is going on. Don't be jealous of them. Don't doubt them. Become that way yourself. You will rejoice. You will not be able to understand why you let yourself continue so long the other way."
Jan Frazier, from Opening the Door

I can say with absolute certainty that I was asleep for several decades of my life. I know I was asleep because I can pinpoint the exact day, the exact moment, and the exact circumstance when I first woke up! Since then I have had lots of small awakenings, and another major awakening. Awakening is like coming out of a fog, when suddenly it clears, and you can see everything clearly.

Some people have woken up lying on a couch, walking through a parking lot to their car, hearing the sound of a bird or something a teacher says, or reading something in particular. Many have woken up in the midst of a terrifying event, or during a personal crisis when their life had hit rock bottom. And for all of them, it was only when they woke up that they realized—they were asleep.

"Most people, even though they don't know it, are asleep. They're born asleep, they live asleep, they marry in their sleep, they breed children in their sleep, they die in their sleep without ever waking up. They live mechanical lives, mechanical thoughts—generally somebody else's—mechanical emotions, mechanical actions, mechanical reactions. They never understand the loveliness and the beauty of this thing that we call human existence."
Anthony de Mello, S.J., from Awareness: Conversations with the Masters

Our mind is mechanical, like a program in a computer, so if we're governed by our mind, then our life is mechanical. Maybe you continually find yourself with not enough money. This is the result of a mechanical mind repeating the same thoughts of "not enough money" over and over again. You empower those thoughts by believing them, and so you continue to experience not having enough money. This is the work of the mind's limiting thoughts, while Awareness is absolute abundance.

When you wake up and begin living your life as Awareness, your life will be beyond anything you can imagine now. You will find the world utterly magnificent, bursting with beauty and loveliness, and you will see with clear eyes that everything is on track, nothing is out of place, and all is well. When our mind is running our life, we're prevented from seeing the world as it really is.

The egoic mind takes issue with most things and objects to them vehemently. Through its ego-centeredness and inability to see the full picture, it will judge, criticize, and find fault, and due to its limited perspective of life, it must perceive problems.

"Waking up is unpleasant, you know. You are nice and comfortable in bed. It is irritating to be woken up. That's the reason the wise guru will not attempt to wake people up. I hope I'm going to be wise here and make no attempt whatsoever to wake you up if you are asleep. It is really none of my business, even though I say to you at times, 'Wake up!'"
Anthony de Mello, S.J., from Awareness: Conversations with the Masters

There's one purpose in life for every one of us—to wake up to who we are, Awareness, and enjoy this incredible spectacle of the world. When you wake up, you will be *in* the world but not *of* the world, which means you will be completely free from the challenges of the world.

As I outlined in the three-step Awareness Practice in the previous chapter, after you've woken up to the truth of Awareness, the final step is to stay consciously as Awareness and not be pulled back into the mind and the ego. Some people wake up suddenly and stay that way permanently, and for others awakening seems to be a process. Everyone, however, says that the process of awakening continues to deepen with no end.

"It isn't any longer possible to say—this is about saints, this is about Zen monks, this is something you must wait lifetimes to have. Or— this is for serious spiritual practitioners, or for people who don't revel in the physical life, or for people who believe a certain way . . .

Know that you can go there, can be there, can live a life that is unencumbered. You do not have to earn this, or deserve it. It's free, already here. It isn't a reward. It's innate."
Jan Frazier, from Opening the Door

Waking up to who you really are is the way out of *all* negativity and the way to permanent happiness. It is the destiny of every human on earth. It is *your* destiny. You can make it your life now!

The Mountain of Consciousness

Many years ago, the Imperator of the European Rose Cross Order shared a metaphor to help me understand the levels of Consciousness and Awareness. He called it "the mountain of consciousness."

If you're at the base of the mountain in the valley, you can't see very far. Your perspective is narrow and limited, and you can't see what's ahead of you or what's around any corner. Because you don't know what's beyond the valley, there is a great fear of the unknown.

As you climb the mountain, you begin to notice changes. Your perspective of life expands as you get higher, because you can see farther and you can see past some of the things that were blocking your view at the bottom of the mountain. Things look different a little higher up because you can see them more clearly, and while still fearful, you're not nearly as fearful as you were in the valley.

Higher again up the mountain, the atmosphere is different, the vegetation is different, and you can see much farther than you could before. Life looks very different here, and because you can now see a lot of things that were hidden from you before, your fear of the unknown is diminishing.

When you reach the top of the mountain, you can see everything in all directions. Nothing whatsoever is hidden from you. Your vision of the world and beyond is fully expanded in every direction. You can see the people in the valley and their limited perspective, and you know from where you are that there's nothing for them to fear. You can also see the people who are at various stages on their way up the mountain, and the various limitations of their perspective. And where you stand, at the top of the mountain, you can see the sheer exquisite beauty and perfection of absolutely everything. You see that nothing is out of place, and there's nothing for anyone to worry about, or be afraid of. The spectacle, the wonder, and the mystery of life that is revealed to you is nothing short of magnificent, and when the people in the valley can see the magnificence of what you can see, they also will be free.

"When we stand on top of a mountain or look at the stars we are sensing infinity, which is what we truly are, and why so many people crave that sense of expansiveness."
David Bingham

"At a higher level of consciousness, none of this personal mind stuff matters at all, for you are standing on the mountaintop of your own being, and all below you are clouds passing. You come to a point where nothing matters at all! Nothing, nothing, nothing! And all is perfection only."
Mooji, from White Fire, *second edition*

Now that you know who you are, you have begun the awakening process! The only obstacle to permanently being who you are is your mind. Your mind is your greatest power in the material world, because it will generate any material thing, event, or circumstance you want, but if you believe its negative thoughts, you will use its creative power against yourself. There's nothing wrong with the mind, it only becomes troublesome when you believe it's who you are.

When your mind tries to speak on your behalf, remember that the voice you hear in your head is not you. Your mind is not even an actual entity, but a process—a mechanical process. It's just made up of thoughts, and the thoughts it produces are coming from programs formed by your beliefs and held in your subconscious mind. The subconscious mind is the storehouse of our beliefs, memory, personality traits, automatic processes, and habits, and its operation is no different from that of a computer; it's completely mechanical.

Your subconscious mind receives information from the conscious mind, which is your thinking mind, and it accepts all the data that the thinking mind puts into it. The subconscious mind doesn't discriminate with any of the information coming into it, but instead accepts everything that *the thinking mind believes is true.*

So basically our mind recycles thoughts according to our beliefs and holds us prisoner with those thoughts by severely limiting our life—until we wake up and see that our thoughts and our mind are not who we are!

"Would you rather play the game of limitation or would you rather be free? That simple question is a key to dropping our obsession with being limited body-minds. If you think you are your body-mind and the stories that you tell yourself and others about being that body-mind, then you would rather play the game of limitation."
Hale Dwoskin, from Happiness Is Free

The first step to freedom is when we understand that our thoughts create our life. What you think is what manifests. You *won't* have the life you want if you give your attention to thoughts of what you *don't want.* And you *will* have the life you want if you give your attention only to thoughts of what you *do want!* When you understand this fully, you become very aware of your thoughts, and it puts you well on the path of awakening, because your awareness of your thoughts not only stops you from believing negative thoughts, but it means you are becoming more aware.

The Secret book and documentary explain the power you have to create your life on all subjects—health, relationships, money, work, happiness, and even the world—through your thoughts. If you don't yet understand the phenomenal power you have through your thoughts, I urge you to get a copy of *The Secret*, or borrow one from a friend or a library. *The Secret* has changed the lives of tens of millions of people, and becoming more aware of your thoughts is an excellent first step in the wonderful process of waking up to what we really are.

CHAPTER 4 *Summary*

- *This life is a dream. The whole world is nothing but a dream-illusion.*

- *In your night dreams your mind creates an entire world and makes everything so real that you don't question it—until you wake up.*

- *The waking state is also only an extremely convincing play that consciousness is producing.*

- *Because the mind is mechanical, if we live from our mind, our life is mechanical.*

- *When our mind is running our life, we're prevented from seeing the world as it really is.*

- *When you wake up, you will be in the world but not of the world.*

- *The Mountain of Consciousness is a metaphor for consciousness: Your perspective of life expands as you get higher. At the top of the mountain, you can see the beauty and perfection of absolutely everything.*

- *Your mind is made up of thoughts, and the thoughts it produces are coming from programs formed by your beliefs and held in your subconscious mind.*

- *The subconscious mind stores our beliefs, memory, personality traits, automatic processes, and habits; its operation is no different from that of a computer.*

- *The first step to freedom is when we understand that our thoughts create our life. What you think is what manifests.*

FREEDOM FROM
THE MIND

"It isn't necessary for the mind to be quiet. All that matters is that you not listen to what it's saying, as if it were true."
Jan Frazier, from The Great Sweetening: Life After Thought

Your mind is an amazing tool to create your life exactly as you want it to be. It is not your psychoanalyst or your therapist, yet we give it that kind of authority over us when we listen to it and believe all its thoughts as though they were true. This one habit of believing our own thoughts robs us of being able to live in the magnificence and glory of our true nature, Awareness. We are prevented from having a life of constant happiness, and a life where everything we need falls into our hands at the perfect time.

Humanity has suffered too much for too long, because of our minds. It's time to delegate our mind to its rightful place so that it is no longer the dictator of our life. When we no longer live from and through the mind, we will begin to live from our true self, Awareness, and our life will truly become heaven on earth, free of suffering and negativity.

"Every problem perceived to be 'out there' is really nothing more than a misperception within your own thinking."
Byron Katie, from Loving What Is

"The most powerful way to remove negativity is to recognize that you are not the mind. Once realized, negativity has nothing to hook to, and it dissolves by itself."
Hale Dwoskin

Most people believe that negative situations come from outside of them; they believe that it's either people, circumstances, or events in the world that have caused the negative situations in their life. But nothing is inherently good or bad, as Shakespeare told us: "There is nothing either good or bad but thinking makes it so."

It's your thoughts about a person, circumstance, or event that's the source of negative situations in your life, not the actual person, circumstance, or event. And so understanding a little of how the mechanics of your mind work will help free you from its erroneous negative judgments, and then you can use it for what it's intended for—to create the life you want.

"Thinking was made to order what you want, not to indulge in it. The mind is there to receive the order and make it appear to you. Thinking isn't needed for anything else because everything else is taken care of by Awareness."
My teacher

"If you would only from this moment on see what you want, that is all that you would get. But you hold in mind the things you do not want. You struggle to eliminate the things you don't want, thereby sustaining them. So, it is necessary to let go of the negative and put in the positive if you want a positive, happy life."
Lester Levenson, from Happiness Is Free, *volumes 1–5*

What exactly is your mind? First, it's important to understand that your mind is not your brain. Your brain doesn't think. Scientists have not been able to find a thought in the brain; they can only see the electrical activity caused by thoughts. Thinking comes from the mind. Your mind is made up entirely of thought. If there's no current thought, there's no mind. It's as simple as that. Your mind can't even hold two thoughts at one time. You know that it's impossible to truly listen to a conversation and read something on your phone at the same time. Your mind can't multitask, as much as you might believe it can.

However, a single thought, whether positive or negative, becomes a powerhouse when you believe it.

"If you prefer to suffer, go on believing your stressful thoughts. But if you'd rather be happy, question them."
Byron Katie, from A Mind at Home with Itself

Most people believe their own thoughts as though they were facts, which explains why life is stressful and challenging for so many. No one pointed out to us that our thoughts are just mental noise, and they are *not* reality. However, if we choose to believe our thoughts, they *will* become our reality!

Mind is the great manifester of our physical life, and it will manifest any and all thoughts we believe, whether they're positive or negative, whether they're thoughts of what we want or what we don't want. Positive thoughts are not harmful to your life because they are close to your true nature; it's negative thoughts that are the cause of our stress and suffering. And so, we need to become particularly aware of negative thoughts.

Because our mind is mechanical, negative thinking can easily become a fixed pattern. If you then listen to and identify with the negative thoughts, you will be drawn in and become lost in your thoughts as though in a hypnotic trance. Your thoughts will constantly take you into your head and away from what is actually happening in the world.

"You believe that you are your mind. This is the delusion. The instrument has taken you over."
Eckhart Tolle, from The Power of Now

It's as though we're playing a virtual reality game and we've forgotten we have a headset on. Because of the challenging circumstances in the virtual reality world, we're stressed and suffering, but if we would just take the headset off, we would realize that the virtual reality world is not real. So it is with our thoughts. When we believe our thoughts, we're immediately caught in an imaginary mind-made movie that's playing inside our head, and we're no longer experiencing the world as it really is.

"All thoughts are lies. The only truth is what is aware of them."
My teacher

"Awareness does the observing; thought does the judging."
Rupert Spira, from The Ashes of Love

Thoughts are also responsible for causing our feelings, and then in turn those feelings will cause more thoughts. When we have a sad thought, it causes a sad feeling, and the sad feeling causes more sad thoughts. We end up looking at life through a veil of sadness, where everything appears sad to us and we cannot see what is *actually* happening in the world.

"Mind is consciousness that has put on limitations. You are originally unlimited and perfect. Later you take on limitations and become the mind."
Ramana Maharshi

If you haven't deliberately programmed your mind to think positively, your mind will constantly throw up negative thoughts that belittle and limit you. "I shouldn't have done that." "What was I thinking?" "That was really dumb." "I'm running out of time." "I can't do that."

"The mind is all, 'No!' 'Too late!' 'Too early!' 'Too fast!' 'Too slow!' The mind never stops."
My teacher

"It's not that the mind is bad. The problem is that it tends to run on automatic, a machine we can't figure out how to turn off. Most of the time, we don't even realize it's running. Its ever-looping content is like elevator music, hardly noticed, like background static that's tuned out. Because the mind goes everywhere we go, the temptation to use it constantly is overwhelming. It runs simply because it can. Like a misapplied hammer, the overactive mind takes random whacks at everything in sight, omitting no opportunity to judge, balk, interpret, identify with, stew over, start a story about."
Jan Frazier, from The Freedom of Being

A mind that's running on automatic will also constantly tell you there's lack in your life and the world—lack of money, lack of health, lack of love, lack of time, lack of resources—and that there's not enough to go around. And if you believe it, that will be what you experience.

Fortunately, your mind is also a magnificent tool. Your positive thoughts of what you want can not only turn your life around but also give you great happiness and joy. If you only thought about what you wanted, your life would be amazing. But many are caught in the addictive pattern of believing negative thoughts, and it is freeing yourself from this loop of negative thinking that is needed and can be done quite easily: your Awareness will help set you free.

Don't Believe the Troublemaker

There's nothing wrong with the mind; the trouble only begins when we believe its negative thoughts. When you feel worried, it's because you are believing worried thoughts. When you feel doubt, it's because you are believing doubtful thoughts. When you feel anxious, upset, disheartened, scared, disappointed, irritated, impatient, revengeful, depressed, hateful, or any negative emotion, it's because you are believing thoughts! And while you hold on to those emotions by continuing to believe your thoughts, your mind will give you even more of the same. A depressed feeling will produce more depressing thoughts, giving you a depressing perspective of people, circumstances, and events, which makes you feel even more depressed, and around and around it goes.

"Thought is so cunning, so clever, that it distorts everything for its own convenience."
J. Krishnamurti, from Freedom from the Known

When we believe the mind's negative thoughts, we get pulled into the mind-made movie, and then we're guaranteed to experience more stress and suffering.

"Self-inflicted misery arises when we believe negative thoughts!"
My teacher

"You are responsible for everything that you feel. They are your feelings, they are your thoughts. You turn them on, you think them, and no one else but you does it—and you act as though you have no control! You turn a faucet that flows on your head and you say, 'Oh someone is getting me all wet.' It's you who's turning on the faucet and getting yourself wet. So, your direction should be taking full responsibility for what's happening to you. Then you'll see by looking in the direction of 'I am doing this' that you are! Then when you see that you're torturing yourself, you'll say, 'My gosh, how stupid can I be?' And you'll stop. Instead of torturing yourself, you'll make yourself happy."
Lester Levenson, from Happiness Is Free, *volumes 1–5*

Taking responsibility for everything in our life also means not blaming anyone or anything else for something that happened. And it means not blaming ourselves. Blaming is just another repetitive program in the mind. The real you never blames—only the mind does. What will set you free from the mind's blaming and criticizing ways is understanding that it's your *mind* that is the sole cause of negative judgments, and to stop believing its negative thoughts.

"As long as you think that the cause of your problem is 'out there'—as long as you think that anyone or anything is responsible for your suffering—the situation is hopeless. It means that you are forever in the role of victim, that you're suffering in paradise."
Byron Katie, from Loving What Is

When we take responsibility for our own life, we no longer allow the ego and mind to play the role of a victim on our behalf.

"No thought ever can dominate that which perceives the thought. Notice what it feels like to realize this. Notice that it feels free. This is what stops the unconscious identification with thoughts. This breaks the chain."
Peter Dziuban, from Simply Notice

It's Awareness that is aware of your thoughts, and it's Awareness that is aware of your emotions. The one who gets upset is not Awareness, the *real* you; the one getting upset is your mind. The one who gets angry, hurt, worried, anxious, or disappointed is not the *real* you, it's your mind. It only feels like you because you believe your mind is you and because you believe your mind's thoughts.

"Like the scrolling text at the bottom of the television screen, let thinking just pass. If attention is not focusing on the text, then you can be fully present to the whole picture."
Kalyani Lawry

The Mind's Three Thoughts

Although our mind arises out of awareness, as everything does, our mind is not an entity or a real thing, even though it sure seems like it is. It's simply a mechanical activity or process, much like a computer program. And just like a computer program, it's repetitive. In fact, it's so repetitive that it only has three different kinds of thoughts.

"The mind measures, compares, and describes. These three things are all the mind does, over and over and over again. Check for yourself with anything you say, or with whatever thought appears. That thought will either be the mind measuring something, comparing something, or describing something."
My teacher

Your mind measures with thoughts like these: "It will take two hours to get there." "I'm going on vacation in one week." "How long will it take for my shipment to arrive?" "I've lost ten pounds." "I don't have enough money."

Your mind is comparing when it thinks thoughts like these: "I prefer an SUV to a sedan." "I like to walk to work instead of taking the bus." "She's smarter than me, and way more talented." "He's going to get the promotion over me, I know it." "Look at her. I wish I had her body." "He's not the person he used to be."

And your mind constantly describes things as if you can't see them. But you can see what's happening in your life very well without mind's constant commentating, and in fact that nonstop chattering prevents you from seeing the world as it really is.

"Our attention focuses mostly on thinking. We become trapped in the interpretations we make and miss out on the fullness of living."
Kalyani Lawry

"The mind makes something of everything that comes along. This has become the default mode. So much so that it little occurs to us that it could be otherwise—that the mind really could forgo the making-something of everything that comes along. Nor does it occur to us that the making-something that keeps the mind so enthralled is the actual cause of suffering. We keep thinking it's the stuff that happens in life that causes suffering."
Jan Frazier, from Opening the Door

When your mind is describing something, it's telling a story. It's an interpretation of the world and reality—it's imagined. Many of the mind's fabricated stories are about *you*, and if believed, those stories can not only cause you stress and suffering but also greatly limit your life. When you believe a negative story, your life will turn into that story! Your mind spins up a negative story about you, you add the power of belief to it, and then your mind projects it into the world for you to experience it. It does it with thoughts like these:

"I'm overwhelmed. I just can't seem to get on top of things."

"I'm no good with money. It seems to slip through my fingers."

"This disease runs in our family."

"I've got a big problem."

"I can't get past the trauma of it. It will affect me for the rest of my life."

"We were together for years, he was the love of my life, so I'll never get over him."

One of the biggest lies our mind has convinced us of is the story that we are a body and a mind. And because we've believed it, it has become our experience. We feel vulnerable, fearful of what might happen to us or others, helpless against life's events and circumstances, and, if that isn't enough, many of us are also burdened with the belief that life will come to an end for us when the body dies. It's ironic that the real you—the Infinite Awareness that you really are—is the direct opposite of that story the mind has told you.

"If you take the way it works, a human being wakes up in the morning and for the first moment there's just stillness; then there's a re-engagement of the mind, the mind kicks in and starts saying, 'What have I got to do today? How old am I? What are my problems? How am I going to stop all these things going wrong?' There is complete identification with the story; you pull your boots on and off you go again."
David Bingham, from Conscious TV

Another story our mind has convinced us of is the story about time. Time is a very convenient tool that enables us to all work from the same calendar and clocks so that we can coordinate our lives with each other and with everything that's happening in the world. But as Einstein discovered, time is relative; ultimately, there's really no such thing as time. Time is an illusion—a mental concept created by the mind.

"If you try to get your hands on time, it's always slipping through your fingers. People are sure time is there, but they can't get hold of it. My feeling is that they can't get hold of it because it isn't there at all."
Julian Barbour, physicist, excerpt from Adam Frank's book About Time

All that really exists is this present moment, and try as you might, you will not be able to find any event or circumstance that happened at any other time than the present moment.

If you try to imagine a world without time, you won't be able to do it because your mind can't comprehend it. Your mind is always either in the past or in the future; it's not aware of this present moment. If you stop and are present right now, you will notice that there is no thought. It's one of the reasons why the mind has been able to prevent so many of us from realizing who we really are, because Awareness can only be recognized in this present moment!

If you don't think your mind creates time, then see if you can find time outside of your mind.

"Try and find any evidence of the past without thought. Try as hard as you can to find any past apart from the current thought of it. It's impossible."

Peter Dziuban, from Consciousness Is All *audiobook*

Now try and find the future without thought. Try really hard.

It's not possible to find any evidence of the past or the future without thought. No one has ever been able to step into the past or into the future. When anything happened in the past, it happened in the present moment. When anything happens in the future, it always happens in the present moment. Check it for yourself. Go back in your memory to when you first rode a bike as a kid. When you were actually riding your bike, were you riding it in the past? Or were you riding your bike in the present moment? When you woke up this morning, did you wake up in the past, or did you wake up in the present moment?

"The past and future cannot be experienced. They can only be mentally processed. Past and future exist only in the form of thought."
Jan Frazier, from The Great Sweetening: Life After Thought

"The only evidence we have of the Earth's past is rocks and fossils. But these are just stable structures in the form of an arrangement of minerals we examine in the present. The point is, all we have are these records and you only have them in this Now."
Julian Barbour, physicist, excerpt from Adam Frank's book About Time

When I was first told that time doesn't exist, my mind went crazy with all kinds of thoughts trying to prove that time does exist! Like, what about old buildings? Aren't they proof there's a past? But when I really examined it, I realized that when the buildings were built they were built in the present moment. And if I am standing looking at the old building, I'm also looking at it in the present moment, and anyone who has looked at the same building also looked at it in the present moment. Eventually as I examined each thought that came up trying to prove time is real, I saw that every one of them was false because there is only the present moment.

"Whether you like it or not, you're in the moment. There's only one moment, it's infinite, and you can't be anywhere else but in it."
My teacher

"Now is not a moment in time, sandwiched between the two vast spaces of past and future. This present Now is the only Now there is—the eternal Now. It has not come from anywhere and is not going anywhere."
Rupert Spira, from The Ashes of Love

If you can just open yourself to the possibility that time is an illusion, it will help set you free.

"The future never comes. Think of that: the future never comes. There is only ever the present. In the present, there is the feeling of not missing life. Of not having anywhere to get to, anything to get done. The present is where it is happening. And it isn't happening anywhere else. It sure as heck isn't happening in the mind, with all the wondering about what's ahead, and the going over (and over) something that has already come and gone."
Jan Frazier, from Opening the Door

"The past is made of memory, the future of imagination. Neither has any existence outside the realm of thought."
Rupert Spira, from The Ashes of Love

The mind constantly fixates on the past and the future, neither of which exists, but which just the same causes us stress and worry. You think to yourself, "I'm running late for our meeting. My boss and work colleagues are going to be furious with me. I was late last week too. I could get fired over this." Instead of believing those thoughts as facts and certainties, be aware that they're *just* flimsy thoughts. They're fabricated stories. But if you believe your mind, it *will* become true.

The mind's storytelling is nothing more than one of its mechanical programs, and yet it has managed to convince most of us that its stories are true—the story that time is real, the story that we're a body and a mind, the story that we are a separate person who is born and dies. All of these things combined play their part in constructing the reality that we experience, but they are all in the mind, and therefore nothing but mental ideas.

"It's not you that people like or dislike; it's their stories of you."
Byron Katie, from A Mind at Home with Itself

Don't believe a story your mind tells you if it's something you don't want; otherwise, you will brand yourself with it. Watch the mechanics of your mind, and don't accept a single story or thought about yourself that is anything but perfection and goodness, because perfection and pure goodness are the fact of what you *really* are!

Awareness Is Your Way Out

"What is a thought? A movement of energy. What is a feeling? A movement of energy."
Peter Lawry, from the talk "Consciousness Unlimited"

What you are, Infinite Awareness, can never be affected by thoughts. So become aware of your thoughts and see them for what they are—just a thought, just energy passing through.

"A thought is like a bird flying by. Let the bird fly past without analyzing it. 'Where are you going? What kind of bird are you? Where's your family? How old are you?' Just let the bird fly past."
My teacher

You don't have to eliminate your mind or go to war with your mind. You will add even more power to your mind if you try to do that. Awareness is your way out of the turmoil of the mind. Just become aware of your thoughts so that you no longer believe them. You can't be aware of your thoughts and believe them at the same time, because Awareness of your thoughts prevents you from identifying with them as though they were true. When you observe your thoughts instead of getting lost in them, you see them for what they are: something that you can either choose to believe, or not.

"Who you are does not need a thought to hear. Doesn't need a thought to see. Doesn't need a thought to sense your body and your surroundings. Who you are is thought free. Awareness is hearing, seeing, sensing everything first without any thought."
My teacher

Remember, your thoughts aren't aware of you; you are the Awareness that is aware of your thoughts.

"When you are willing to really look at how seriously you take yourself, your mind can start to feel at peace, with a little warm breeze drifting around in there. Who you have held on to as being you—your opinions, your desires, fears, what you're invested in—has gotten a little hazy around the edges. Life is feeling strangely easy. Joyful even. What happens just . . . happens. You're okay with it, really and truly okay. No opinion about it floats across the radar screen. It's gotten very quiet inside your head. You realize how very hard you've been working, your entire well-meaning life. Life just began for you."
Jan Frazier, from Opening the Door

CHAPTER 5 *Summary*

- *The habit of believing our own thoughts robs us of being able to live in the magnificence and glory of who we really are.*

- *It's your thoughts about a person, circumstance, or event that's the source of negative situations in your life, not the actual person, circumstance, or event.*

- *Thinking was made to order what you want. Thinking isn't needed for anything else because everything else is taken care of by Awareness.*

- *Your mind is not your brain. Your brain doesn't think. Thoughts come from your mind.*

- *Your mind is made up entirely of thought. If there's no current thought, there's no mind.*

- *Most people believe their own thoughts as though they were facts, which explains why life is stressful and challenging for so many.*

- *It's negative thoughts that are the cause of our stress and suffering, so we need to become particularly aware of negative thoughts.*

- *When we believe our thoughts, we're immediately caught in an imaginary mind-made movie that's playing inside our head, and we're no longer experiencing the world as it really is.*

- *Thoughts are also responsible for causing our feelings, and then in turn our feelings will cause more thoughts.*

- *There's nothing wrong with the mind; the trouble only begins when we believe its negative thoughts.*

- *The one who gets angry, hurt, worried, anxious, or disappointed is not the* real *you. It's your mind.*

- *The mind only has three different kinds of thoughts. The mind measures, compares, and describes.*

- *One of the biggest lies our mind has convinced us of is the story that we are a body and a mind.*

- *Another story our mind has convinced us of is the story about time. Time is an illusion—a mental concept created by the mind.*

- *All that really exists is this present moment. Past and future exist only in the form of thought.*

- *You don't have to eliminate your mind or go to war with your mind. Awareness is your way out of the turmoil of the mind.*

- *When you observe your thoughts instead of getting lost in them, you see them for what they are: something separate from you that you can either choose to believe, or not.*

UNDERSTANDING THE POWER OF FEELINGS

It is possible to live your life without ever being thrown about by negative feelings again. When you live from the Awareness that you are, negative feelings won't affect you in the same way as they do now. The real you is pure happiness at all times and under all conditions. It can be hard to imagine that you can bring an end to negative feelings affecting you, but you will discover for yourself that you can.

"Negative feelings are destructive. What we are is constructive."
My teacher

Through practicing the methods shared in this book, I don't suffer from extreme negative feelings anymore. If any negative feeling appears, it's quite soft, I notice it immediately, and it dissolves on the spot. Earlier in my life, I used to be thrown about by negative feelings as if I had just stepped into a hurricane. But after I discovered The Secret, I became acutely aware of how I'm feeling from one moment to the next. And if you're aware of how you're feeling, it's just one more simple step, as you will discover, to dissolving negative feelings for good. When you are free of all negative feelings, what remains is the Infinite Awareness that you are, and your life will be absolutely breathtaking.

"Once you realize how effortless the highest way of life is, it takes tremendous effort to assume the opposite."
Lester Levenson

It helps to diminish their power over you if you understand what feelings really are.

Feelings (and thoughts and sensations) are simply a movement of energy. Energy vibrates, which means feelings, like thoughts, also vibrate. Different feelings vibrate at different frequencies. Good feelings vibrate at higher frequencies, and they're very beneficial to the body and positively affect the circumstances surrounding your life. Your positive feelings also benefit all other beings and the planet as a whole. Negative feelings vibrate at low frequencies, and they're detrimental to the body, to your life circumstances, other beings, and the planet. But where do feelings come from in the first place?

Thoughts create feelings. The kinds of thoughts you have will create the same kinds of feelings. After having happy thoughts, you feel happy. And once you're feeling happy, it's not possible to have angry thoughts at the same time. Happy thoughts cause happy feelings, which cause more happy thoughts. Likewise, if you feel angry, that feeling has come from having had angry thoughts. Thoughts and feelings always match; thoughts and feelings are two sides of the one coin.

If a situation arises and you allow negative thoughts and feelings to take over you, you will likely continue to experience one thing going wrong after another in your day. However, when you feel good, your day will have one good thing following after another. What you feel inside will match precisely with what you experience in the world around you.

"You now know that nothing comes into existence from the outside, and that everything first comes from thinking and feeling it on the inside."

From The Secret

Positive Feelings

Have you noticed that all good feelings require zero effort? When you're feeling good, you feel as light as a feather, and you feel as though you have an unlimited supply of energy. If you become sensitive to how you're feeling, you will notice the positive effect those good feelings are having on your body and mind.

Feeling good doesn't mean you're like a cheerleader at a football game, jumping up and down with excitement. As you no doubt would have experienced, if you get overexcited, you dissipate all your energy, and you're exhausted afterward.

Feeling good is like how you feel at the end of a big day that went really well, or when you're chilled out on vacation, or when you've exercised hard, had a shower, and then sat down to enjoy dinner or your favorite show. You feel relaxed. You feel a sense of relief. You let go, and you feel a peaceful happiness. You know those times when you say, "Ahh, this is nice"? This is what feeling good feels like. If you could let go of your white-knuckle grip on life, you would automatically feel this good, because feeling good is your true nature. In fact, whenever you feel good, it means you must have let go of bad feelings, enabling good feelings to naturally appear.

"Good feelings are to be enjoyed. They are the expression of joy and take us back to joy, which is our true nature. Just enjoy them; be one with them."

Francis Lucille, from The Perfume of Silence

Positive and good feelings are a result of saying "Yes" to what is happening in life. Positive feelings come from "Yes, I want that," "Yes, that would be nice," "Yes, that's good," "Yes, I love this," or "Yes, that sounds great."

There's not a problem with positive or good feelings. Happiness and good feelings, after all, come from Awareness. Bask in good feelings, milk them, and fall in love with them.

Negative Feelings

Negative feelings are a result of you thinking or saying "No!" about something that's happening. Negative feelings come from "No, I don't want this!" It could be something hurtful a person said or did; someone disagreeing with you; or a circumstance, big or small, that didn't go the way you wanted, such as having an argument; running late; a health issue; a relationship breakup; mounting debt; losing your phone; heavy traffic; late deliveries; items out of stock; the weather too hot or too cold; issues with the government; late or canceled flights; no parking spaces; or long lines at the supermarket, bank, or airport.

When you think or say, "No! I don't want this," it immediately causes resistance in you, and it's the resistance that produces the bad feelings. And then, as if it isn't enough that we resist a situation, we go ahead and resist the bad feelings as well. We find ourselves feeling even worse, trapped in a web of bad feelings caused not actually by anything happening in the outside world, but by our own reactions. Our resistance to what is happening and our negative feelings not only hold the situation we don't want firmly to us, but also drain our body of energy and even impact our immune system!

"Feeling sad about anything is holding on to it. Say, 'This is something I have to let go of,' and immediately you will feel better."
Lester Levenson, from Happiness Is Free, *volumes 1–5*

Positive feelings are completely effortless because they're the true nature of Awareness. We are made of positive feelings; we are made of joy, happiness, and love. Negative feelings require a huge amount of energy to maintain, and it's the reason why we're exhausted if we lose it during the day. A bout of negative emotion such as when we lose our temper will wipe us out, because it has taken so much effort and energy to build it up and sustain it. It takes effort because it's not who we are; when we feel any negative feelings, in that moment we are fighting against who we are.

"'Me' maintenance takes a lot of energy."
Peter Lawry

"It takes a lot of energy to be a person. It takes no energy to be yourself."
Mooji

"After you let go of enough ego, you naturally feel the peace and joy of your Self."
Lester Levenson, from Happiness Is Free, *volumes 1–5*

Positive, good feelings occur naturally in the absence of negative feelings. You don't have to make any effort to have positive feelings. All you have to do is let go of bad feelings, and then you'll naturally feel happy and really good.

"Love is effortless, and hate requires much effort."
Lester Levenson, from Happiness Is Free, *volumes 1–5*

Buried Feelings

"Much of the emotional burden you now carry began life as a pushed-away feeling."
Jan Frazier, from The Freedom of Being

From the time we were young children, we have unconsciously suppressed countless bad feelings, which are now stored in our subconscious mind. The bad feelings remain buried in the subconscious mind, diminishing our energy and our life. All of that energy is trapped in the body, and it's this trapped energy that plays havoc on the body's health and on the circumstances of our life.

Bad feelings or negative feelings are the only feelings we suppress and bury, and so suppressed feelings and negative feelings are actually the same thing. The anger that you feel when you get angry is the very same suppressed anger coming from deep inside you.

In addition, suppressed negative feelings have many negative thoughts attached to them, which are the thoughts that made us feel bad in the first place as well as all the thoughts we've had ever since that are connected to the negative feeling. The thoughts that are attached to the suppressed negative feeling keep us trapped in the mind by continually recycling themselves, detrimentally affecting our life and preventing us from realizing our true self.

Babies and children under about three years of age don't suppress emotions because they're naturally living in their true nature of Awareness, so they automatically let go of emotions. It's the reason why you see babies and toddlers go from tears to smiles and laughter in seconds; they don't resist any emotion.

"By the time we are labeled adults, we are so good at suppressing that most of the time it is totally second nature. We become as good or better at suppressing as we originally were at letting go. In fact, we have suppressed so much of our emotional energy that we are all a little like walking time bombs. Often, we don't even know that we have suppressed our true emotional reactions until it is too late: our body shows signs of stress-related illnesses, our shoulders are stuck in our ears, our stomach is in knots, or we have exploded and said or done something that we now regret."
Hale Dwoskin, from The Sedona Method

When you have a negative experience that causes bad feelings, unless you let go of the bad feeling completely, it ends up being pushed down and suppressed inside you.

Even when you might think that you got something off your chest, or that the situation that upset you was resolved, unless you specifically let go of the negative feeling, it will remain with you, suppressed in your subconscious mind.

"The expression of negative feelings allows just enough of the inner pressure to be let out so that the remainder can then be suppressed. This is a very important point to understand, for many people in society today believe that expressing their feelings frees them from the feelings. The facts are to the contrary."
Dr. David R. Hawkins, from Letting Go

So, letting off steam or venting isn't the answer. That will just add more energy to our already suppressed emotion, because expressed feelings get suppressed too.

Sometimes we also *deliberately* repress our bad feelings, and they also are pushed down into the subconscious. We deliberately repress our emotions when we push aside feelings that make us uncomfortable, like grief and sadness, or when we stifle feelings like anger.

"Suppression is keeping a lid on our emotions, pushing them back down, denying them, repressing them and pretending that they don't exist. Any emotion that comes into awareness that is not let go of is automatically stored in a part of our mind called the subconscious. A big part of how we suppress our emotions is by escaping them."
Hale Dwoskin, from The Sedona Method

Imagine you have a disappointing experience with a family member or friend. Your opinion is that the person let you down, and you're disappointed in them. That feeling of disappointment remains suppressed within you, and the pressure of the trapped emotional energy builds up until some of it has to be released. The suppressed disappointment has to find an outlet to take some pressure off the body, so it will find people, circumstances, or events that will disappoint you, enabling some of its built-up energy to be released. This applies to every negative feeling that you have ever suppressed, and most of us have suppressed the whole gamut of negative feelings. If you've felt it, you've suppressed it.

If you ever feel annoyed, then you know that annoyance was already suppressed inside you. If you didn't have it suppressed inside you already, you wouldn't be able to feel annoyed about anything. So, any time you feel annoyed it's the original annoyance that you felt and suppressed that's coming out. And it's the case with every negative feeling, whether that be anger, frustration, irritation, revenge, hate, depression, grief, despair, jealousy, guilt, shame, impatience, disillusionment, disappointment, aggravation, or being overwhelmed. Unfortunately, we suppressed many negative feelings as children because in our innocence they were too hurtful for us to handle, and then as life went on, it became a habit to push our feelings away instead of letting them be. So, we've likely all had a lifetime of suppressing or repressing bad feelings.

Your mind will cover up the true cause of a bad feeling by using projection to convince you that your feeling was caused by something in the world.

"[The mind] blames events or other people for 'causing' a feeling and views itself as the helpless innocent victim of external causes. 'They made me angry,' 'He got me upset,' 'It scared me,' 'World events are the cause of my anxiety.' Actually, it's the exact opposite. The suppressed and repressed feelings seek an outlet and utilize the events as triggers and excuses to vent themselves. We are like pressure-cookers ready to release steam when the opportunity arises. Our triggers are set and ready to go off. In psychiatry this mechanism is called displacement. It is because we are angry that events 'make' us angry."
Dr. David R. Hawkins, from Letting Go

Don't you feel exactly like a pressure cooker when a bad feeling like anger sweeps over you strongly and really fast? If you know of someone who suffers from frequent anger, it means that they've suppressed a lot of anger, most likely in the earlier years of their life. They're also sure to believe that it's other people or circumstances that bring on a bout of their anger, but most definitely it's their suppressed anger that is the sole cause.

"The real source of 'stress' is actually internal; it is not external, as people would like to believe. The readiness to react with fear, for instance, depends on how much fear is already present within to be triggered by a stimulus. The more fear we have on the inside, the more our perception of the world is changed to a fearful, guarded expectancy. To the fearful person, this world is a terrifying place. To the angry person, this world is a chaos of frustration and vexation. To the guilty person, it is a world of temptation and sin, which they see everywhere. What we are holding inside colors our world. If we let go of guilt, we will see innocence; however, a guilt-ridden person will see only evil."
Dr. David R. Hawkins, from Letting Go

So, when you next experience a negative feeling sweeping over you, remember that no matter how it might appear to you, you're experiencing it because it is *already* inside you—not because an outside person or circumstance caused it.

You would think we would have worked this out, wouldn't you? After all, it's clear from our experience that negative feelings arise from *inside* our body. Not one of us has ever walked down a street and had to dodge negative feelings flying toward us! You'll never find a negative feeling outside of your body, or anybody else's body. It is our *reaction* to a person, circumstance, or event that is the cause of negative feelings, not the actual person, circumstance, or event.

Honey, I Shrunk Myself

Negative feelings are energized even further when we believe that a negative feeling is who we are. How can we be a feeling? Yet when we identify with a feeling, it means we have shrunk our Infinite Self right down, because we're allowing ourselves to be ruled by one puny little feeling.

"Thoughts and emotions seem powerful because we give them energy. By letting them rise and fall of their own, they simply move on."
Kalyani Lawry

"It is not true to say, 'I am sad.' We should say instead, 'At this moment a feeling of sadness is flowing through me.' If we just let the feeling of sadness flow, we automatically and unknowingly take our stand in that which is not flowing."
Francis Lucille, from The Perfume of Silence

Ask yourself: Are you the feeling of sadness, or are you the one that's aware of the sadness?
You're the one that's aware of the sadness.
Were you here before the sadness came?
I'm pretty sure you were.
Will you still remain after the sadness leaves?
I hope you will still be here.
Will you lose a bit of yourself when the sadness goes?
I sure hope not.

Yes, you were here before the sadness came, and yes, you're here after it leaves, fully intact, because you are not sadness. Sadness is something you're *aware of*. It's not at all who you are. Don't let a feeling shrink you down to the size of a pea, when you are the Infinite Being that holds the Universe in place!

"Stop acting so small. You are the universe in ecstatic motion."
Rumi

My teacher suggested that I question *every* negative feeling with:

"Am I that, or am I the one that is aware of it?"

This question immediately takes most of the power out of the feeling because it stops you from identifying with it.

"See that thoughts and feelings are like a train that enters a station and then leaves; be like the station, not like a passenger."
Rupert Spira, from The Ashes of Love

Notice that feelings appear and then disappear, and that it's you, Awareness, that is aware of them when they first appear and aware of them when they disappear.

"Negative feelings are in you, not in reality. Never identify with that feeling. It has nothing to do with the 'I.' Don't define your essential self in terms of that feeling. Don't say, 'I am depressed.' If you want to say, 'It is depressed,' that's all right. If you want to say, 'Depression is there,' that's fine; if you want to say, 'Gloominess is there,' that's fine. But not: 'I am gloomy.' You're defining yourself in terms of the feeling. That's your illusion; that's your mistake. There is a depression there right now, there are hurt feelings there right now, but let it be, leave it alone. It will pass. Everything passes, everything."

Anthony de Mello, S.J., from Awareness: Conversations with the Masters

"Say to your mind, 'Get as worked up or depressed as you want. I am only ever going to observe or ignore you, but I am not going to join you.'"

Mooji

It's an Inside Job

"Imagine a patient who goes to a doctor and tells him what he is suffering from. The doctor says, 'Very well, I've understood your symptoms. Do you know what I will do? I will prescribe a medicine for your neighbor!' The patient replies, 'Thank you very much, Doctor, that makes me feel much better.' Isn't that absurd? But that's what we all do. The person who is asleep always thinks he'll feel better if somebody else changes. You're suffering because you are asleep, but you're thinking, 'How wonderful life would be if somebody else would change; how wonderful life would be if my neighbor changed, my wife changed, my boss changed.'"

Anthony de Mello, S.J., from Awareness: Conversations with the Masters

Don't expect people, circumstances, and events to change for you to feel better, because none of them ever will. You'll never be happy if you wait for the world to change according to your desires or your expectations. To change how you feel in any given moment is always an inside job.

"We spend all our time and energy trying to change external circumstances, trying to change our spouses, our bosses, our friends, our enemies, and everybody else. We don't have to change anything. Negative feelings are in you. No person on earth has the power

to make you unhappy . . . Nobody told you this; they told you the opposite."
Anthony de Mello, S.J., from Awareness: Conversations with the Masters

Negative feelings are self-inflicted. We're the ones who cause our own stress and upset, as much as we would like to think that our stress and upset are inflicted upon us from the world around us.

"The actions of others do not have the power to grant you or deny you peace."
Jac O'Keeffe

"No event justifies a negative feeling. There is no situation in the world that justifies a negative feeling. That's what all our mystics have been crying themselves hoarse to tell us. But nobody listens. The negative feeling is in you."
Anthony de Mello, S.J., from Awareness: Conversations with the Masters

It's *good news* that we inflict negative feelings on ourselves, because it means we have the power to stop doing it! And when we suffer enough with those bad feelings, we will want to find a way out. Nothing teaches us to look for a way out more than unhappiness and being miserable. Even better news, there's a simple way to end bad feelings—for good.

CHAPTER 6 *Summary*

- *When you are free of all negative feelings, what remains is the Infinite Awareness that you are, and your life will be absolutely breathtaking.*

- *Thoughts create feelings. The kinds of thoughts you have will create the same kinds of feelings.*

- *What you feel inside will match precisely with your experience in the outside world.*

- *Feeling good is your true nature. Whenever you feel good, it means you must have let go of bad feelings, enabling good feelings to naturally arise.*

- *Positive and good feelings are a result of saying "Yes" to what is happening in life. Negative feelings are a result of thinking or saying "No!" about what is happening in life.*

- *Positive feelings are completely effortless because they're our true nature. Negative feelings require a huge amount of energy to maintain.*

- *From the time we were children we have unconsciously suppressed countless negative feelings, which are now stored in our subconscious mind.*

- *When you have a negative experience that causes bad feelings, unless you let go of the negative feeling completely, it ends up being pushed down and suppressed inside you.*

- *Letting off steam or venting isn't the answer. That will just add more energy to our already suppressed emotion, because expressed feelings get suppressed too.*

- *A suppressed feeling will find an outlet to take some pressure off the body, so it will find people, circumstances, or events to enable some of its built-up energy to be released.*

- *When you next experience a negative emotion sweeping over you, remember that no matter how it might appear to you, you're experiencing it because it is already inside you—not because an outside person or circumstance caused it.*

- *Negative feelings are energized even further when we believe that a negative feeling is who we are.*

- *Question every negative feeling with: "Am I that, or am I the one that is aware of it?"*

- *Notice that feelings appear and then disappear, and that it's you, Awareness, that is aware of them coming and going.*

- *Don't expect people, circumstances, and events to change for you to feel better. To change how you feel in any given moment is always an inside job.*

The End of Negative Feelings

"The only thing standing between you and what you are is a thought or a feeling. It's very simple."
My teacher

Happiness is your natural state, so if you don't feel happy right now, then you have a negative feeling that is stopping that happiness from being present within you. This chapter has various practices that will help end negative feelings that have had you wrapped in their repetitive loop. When you are free from them, you will finally live your life in your natural state of sheer joy and happiness—a life more spectacular than anything you have lived up until now.

"The first thing you need to do is get in touch with negative feelings that you're not even aware of. Lots of people have negative feelings they're not aware of. Lots of people are depressed and they're not aware they are depressed. It's only when they make contact with joy that they understand how depressed they were. The first thing you need is awareness of your negative feelings. What negative feelings? Gloominess, for instance. You're feeling gloomy and moody. You feel self-hatred or guilt. You feel that life is pointless, that it makes no sense; you've got hurt feelings, you're feeling nervous and tense. Get in touch with those feelings first."
Anthony de Mello, S.J., from Awareness: Conversations with the Masters

You don't need to know the name of the negative feeling you have, because sometimes it can be hard to pinpoint exactly what you're feeling. All you need to know is that if the feeling isn't a happy feeling, it's a negative feeling, and that negative feeling is holding back your life and preventing you from living in constant happiness.

Just be aware of the negative feeling without resisting it, expressing it, or judging it in any way, and recognize that it's just a feeling. Do not make any attempt to change the feeling. When you stop wanting to get rid of the feeling, and you stop resisting it, the energy will be released and the feeling can disappear.

"If you stop resisting an emotion, it cannot stand."
Rupert Spira, from the talk "Rest in Your Being"

We've convinced ourselves that if we resist bad feelings we make them go away, but instead we are guaranteeing that we will experience them over and over again. As the psychiatrist Carl Jung said, "Whatever you resist, persists." Take away resistance and any negative feeling, no matter how strong, passes through the body quickly.

My teacher showed me that when you place the palm of your hand against someone else's palm and each of you push against the other's hand, you will feel resistance. If the other person stops pushing with their hand, immediately both hands drop. If you can, experiment with this with a friend or family member, because experiencing it for yourself will make it crystal clear. This is exactly what happens when you stop resisting a negative emotion—it drops away.

To stop resisting a negative feeling, you have to *allow* the feeling to be present without trying to change it. Just be *aware* of the feeling. Relax and don't tense up against it, because that's resisting it. Ironically, you let the feeling go by relaxing and allowing it to be there, without wanting to change it or get rid of it, without wanting to make it different or do anything about it. Let the feeling be there, and that allows the energy of it to be released. It's the very opposite to what we've always done, which explains why we have so many suppressed negative emotions.

"Resistance is quite insidious. It's one of the main things that stop us from having, doing, and being what we want in life."
Hale Dwoskin, from The Sedona Method

The energy behind a negative feeling will naturally release when you allow the feeling to be present. It's an automatic process. All you have to do is be aware of the feeling, allow it to be present, and not try to push it away, change it, control it, or get rid of it. When you fully allow the feeling, the energy of the feeling passes very quickly and at the same time it takes a big chunk of the suppressed feeling with it. For example, if you don't resist an angry feeling when it appears and you allow it to be present, it will quickly move through you, taking with it some of the original anger that you suppressed early in your life.

"Don't be afraid of feelings—let them come up and be released."
Shakti Caterina Maggi

When we notice a feeling and allow it to be just as it is, we're no longer suppressing or repressing it. We've finally begun to free the suppressed feeling. Even a bout of extreme anger can fall away in under a minute if we are simply aware of it, allow it to be there, and don't resist it.

"When we strongly identify with negative emotions, rather than observing them, they can very quickly drain our energy supply. By remaining present and learning how to dis-identify from the emotions, we can reclaim control of our energy supply which then becomes available to enhance our life experience."
David Bingham

The following practices I'm about to share are the most effective methods I know of to permanently release negative feelings, including all of the suppressed negative feelings that you have accrued throughout your whole life. And when they've gone, you won't be affected by negative feelings the way you once were, your health will skyrocket, and so will your finances, your relationships, and your entire life. Even better, once the negative feelings are all gone, you will be standing unimpeded in the joy and happiness of Infinite Awareness. Whatever you want will appear in your life effortlessly. You will be having the experience of a human being while being the Infinite Being that you actually are.

"When everything that can be let go of is let go of, what remains is what we desire above all else."
Rupert Spira, from The Ashes of Love

Welcoming

The brilliant teacher and ex-physicist Francis Lucille describes one method of releasing negative feelings as "welcoming." Welcoming has proven to be one of the most powerful practices I have ever done in my life. This practice eradicates negative feelings once and for all.

(It's also worth noting that the situation or circumstance that caused the negative feeling in the first place will also change when you welcome the negative feeling. This is due to you releasing the feeling you have about the situation.)

Welcoming is the opposite of resisting. Resistance says to a negative feeling, "No, I don't want this!" And welcoming says, "Yes, you are welcome here." Awareness is always welcoming of everything. No negative feeling, no matter how strong, can stand up against the welcoming of Awareness. In fact, no negativity whatsoever can stand up against the welcoming of Awareness.

It seems counterintuitive to welcome something you don't want, but it's resistance that holds what you don't want to you, and welcoming stops you from resisting! It can be challenging not to resist or tense up against a negative feeling, but when you open your attention and welcome the feeling, miraculously the resistance ceases, and the negative feeling—which is just energy—dissolves. The situation that you were resisting will then be able to change.

Remember, opening your attention is like zooming out with a camera lens so you're not focused on any detail with your mind. Make sure that you don't focus into the feeling. That will make it stronger, because the mind *increases* anything we focus on. Notice the feeling, but don't focus into it. Keep your attention wide.

Teacher Hale Dwoskin suggests that, in the beginning, it can be helpful to open your arms out to the side of your body when you open your attention. Open your arms as though you are welcoming somebody you love whom you're about to embrace. This helps you open your heart (we have a tendency to keep the heart area of our body permanently contracted, without realizing we're doing it). I consciously open my heart when I welcome anything in life that I do not want.

My teacher says that when we're welcoming, we are being our true self, Awareness, because welcoming is our very nature. In fact, the Infinite Awareness that you are is so welcoming that negative feelings can't possibly remain in its presence. Quite simply, when you welcome anything negative, you allow it to dissolve back into its source—You, Awareness! And so when you welcome a negative feeling you are tapping into your infinite power to dissolve it.

Teacher Francis Lucille says that as we become more established in welcoming, we realize that welcoming is not really an activity of its own; rather, welcoming stops the activity of resistance. Initially we think that welcoming is something we do, and as we practice it more, we realize that it's actually *stopping* us from doing something many of us do automatically—resisting.

"The feeling evaporates because it's only energy, so when a feeling arises, notice it is only energy and welcome it. It has arisen because you're ready to be free of it."
My teacher

What Hurts You, Blesses You

Some years ago, I found myself in a state of depression. At that time I didn't know most of the things that I'm sharing in this book, but fortunately, I knew how I had brought about depression. My daughter was very sick at the time and I feared for her life, and I had one terrifying thought after another. Because I believed those fearful thoughts, in a few months they sent me spiraling down into depression.

"Feelings like anger or sadness exist only to alert you to the fact that you're believing your own stories."
Byron Katie, from A Mind at Home with Itself

To lift myself out of the depression I tried to think positive thoughts and thoughts of gratitude, but what I discovered is that our thoughts have very little power in the depths of depression. It's a safety mechanism that protects us from our thoughts manifesting when we're down really low in despair or depression. So, with the failure of my usual way to turn things around, I had to find another way.

I decided that if I couldn't override the depression with positive thoughts, I would just stop resisting the depression, because I knew that "what you resist persists." So I closed my eyes and focused inside my body where the depression seemed to dwell. I opened myself up to that black cloud of depression as if I were stretching my arms out to welcome it, and as if I were embracing it by putting my arms around it, just as you would greet someone you love dearly and haven't seen in a long time. I opened up my heart and loved the depression as best I could and pulled it in close toward me. For a few seconds it worsened, and then all of a sudden it became lighter and lighter, and then completely dissolved. In a matter of seconds it had gone—just like that. The relief was exquisite.

A few hours later the feeling of depression came back, but it was much less intense than before. I followed the same process, and I continued to do it whenever the depression reappeared. Each time I did the practice, the depression got weaker and weaker, and in just a few days it had totally gone.

"The moment you accept what troubles you've been given, the door will open."
Rumi

I know without any doubt that I will never suffer from depression again. It has left my body permanently.

If I can do this with depression, you can do it with any negative feeling. When you do it yourself, you will understand the process much better. Dissolving a negative emotion when it's in full flight is the best feeling in the world. Instead of resisting the feeling of depression, which only made it worse and held it to me, I did the opposite. In my own way, even though I didn't know it at the time, I had intuitively welcomed the negative feeling of depression.

Since that time, I have used the same practice for any negative feelings that have arisen, for negative thoughts, and I have also used it for any painful sensations in the body, like a cramp in the foot or a headache. I've found that bodily sensations can dissolve as quickly as negative feelings when they're not resisted.

Use the welcoming process for anything that makes you feel bad, any negative thoughts or stories, negative feelings, painful sensations or memories, and limiting beliefs. Welcoming frees you from emotional bondage and allows your life to change for the better in every possible way.

"When we love our hate, we stop hating. Love always wins. To love hatred means to welcome it. It doesn't mean that we should do what it tells us to do, but we shouldn't suppress it either. When we love hatred, we put ourselves out of the process of hatred, and love begins."

Francis Lucille, from The Perfume of Silence

Negative feelings like fear can be immensely uncomfortable, or even terrifying, which is why many of us have developed the habit of automatically suppressing them rather than facing them. But they have fooled us. When we allow any negative feeling to be present, welcoming it without trying to push it away, it may feel overwhelming for a couple of seconds as it intensifies, but then it completely disappears.

When you have allowed a bad feeling to be present and you haven't suppressed it, that feeling will never be as strong in you again. You have weakened it, and it is now on its way out. A few more times of allowing the feeling to be present and it will be released from your body. Watch then how much happiness floods into your body, and how much goodness floods into your life from just one negative feeling being released.

"Sometimes we surrender a feeling and we notice that it returns or continues. This is because there is more of it yet to be surrendered. We have stuffed these feelings all of our lives and there can be a lot of energy pushed down that needs to come up and be acknowledged. When surrender occurs, there is an immediate lighter, happier feeling, almost like a 'high.'"

Dr. David R. Hawkins, from Letting Go

The relief that you will feel from releasing negative feelings from the body is exquisite. And with every released negative feeling your body will become lighter, your life more effortless, and you will find your happiness expanding. You also gain momentum the more you do it, and it becomes easier and easier to release negative feelings. You'll reach a point where most negative feelings dissolve instantly, because they are automatically released the moment you're aware of them. This is the infinite power of Awareness.

"Releasing is like breathing—it's natural. Inhale and exhale."
My teacher

"That's what every uncomfortable feeling is for—that's what pain is for, what money is for, what everything in the world is for: your self-realization."
Byron Katie, from Loving What Is

Every negative feeling is there to direct you back home to who you are. They alert you to the fact that you're believing stories that are not true, so you can welcome those feelings and live your life as the magnificent Awareness that you truly are. Isn't it ironic that negative feelings, the one thing we do everything we can to avoid, are the very thing that will liberate us?

"What hurts you, blesses you. Darkness is your candle."
Rumi

Use every negative emotion that appears as an opportunity to permanently free yourself from that negative emotion. As my teacher said, a negative emotion only arises when you're ready to be free of it. Welcome the emotion, without trying to change it or get rid of it. You are the Infinite Being, and welcoming is your very nature. Welcome every negative feeling until you are free of them all forever.

"It is possible to be in very 'peaceful' surroundings and yet be tormented, and it is possible to be in dangerous, noisy, negative-feeling surroundings and yet be entirely at peace."
Jan Frazier, from Opening the Door

How do you welcome feelings about subjects that you have a strong opinion about, or a strong stance against, like cruelty to animals?

Understand that the bad feelings you feel around that subject are causing *you* harm and are not helping what you care about. Welcome the sensations and feelings that the subject may evoke in you. Welcome your disapproval, welcome the feelings of unfairness and injustice. Keep welcoming until there is no sensation or feeling left when you think of the subject.

You might think that you don't want to stop feeling the pain about a subject, because then you'll stop caring about it. But this is a story the mind is telling you, and the very opposite is true. Your strong resistance to a subject energizes it, adding a lot of energy and power that makes it bigger. So when you release your negative feelings around it, you are releasing all the energy you have focused on it, and you are *disempowering* the circumstances surrounding the subject. Without that negative emotion, your love and compassion, which will naturally arise in place of the negative emotions, have atomic power, and they can make a huge difference in the world.

Let me tell you about Lester Levenson. Lester became enlightened through releasing all of his negative emotions and beliefs over a three-month period. Prior to this, Lester had many health problems, including depression, migraine headaches, gastrointestinal imbalances, jaundice, an enlarged liver, kidney stones, spleen trouble, hyperacidity, ulcers that had perforated his stomach and formed lesions, and coronary heart disease.

One by one every disease and affliction disappeared as Lester released his suppressed negative feelings. Lester called his practice of releasing negative emotions "The Method," and later, under the guardianship of one of his students, Hale Dwoskin, who is featured in both *The Secret* and this book, it would become known as "The Sedona Method."

"I was letting go and undoing the hell I had created. By squaring all with love, trying to love rather than trying to be loved, and by taking responsibility for all that was happening to me; finding my subconscious thought and correcting it, I became freer and freer, happier and happier."
Lester Levenson

"Think of one painful memory from early life, one terrible regret that has been hidden. Look at all the years and years of thoughts associated with that single event. If we could surrender the underlying painful feeling, all of those thoughts would disappear instantly, and we would forget the event."
Dr. David R. Hawkins, from Letting Go

When we release or welcome a suppressed feeling evoked from a memory, no matter how far back that memory goes, all the hundreds and thousands of thoughts attached to that memory will be released with the feeling. There's nothing better than doing this! The lightness, the happiness, and the "high" you feel as you release the feelings attached to painful memories cannot be described, not to mention how completely your life changes. You will know with certainty that those suppressed feelings have been affecting the health of your body when you release them. And when you see all the circumstances of your life begin to change for the better, as they most definitely will, you will know through your own experience that those feelings were holding your life back too.

I once did this practice on a hurtful childhood experience that had stayed with me all my life, and I can now no longer remember what the experience was; I only remember releasing it. When I released the hurtful feeling that the memory evoked, it took all of the thoughts of the memory with it, so much so that the memory itself vanished!

Hurtful memories are heavy burdens for us to carry; they get in the way of us having the life we deserve, and they're not who we are. You can free yourself of painful memories.

"Notice the *feeling* behind every thought and it will dissolve. It's a self-cleaning mechanism. Use the shortcut of dissolving feelings to dissolve hundreds of negative thoughts by welcoming the feeling."
My teacher

It's inspiring to know that releasing just one negative feeling will take out hundreds if not thousands of negative thoughts with it. As you dissolve your negative feelings, you take out thoughts of doubt, un-worthiness, needing approval from others, insecurity, lacking confi-dence, and every other kind of negative thought that holds you back from a life filled with wonder and continuous happiness. With every negative feeling that is released, your life will soar.

The Super Practice

I want to share with you an invaluable practice that my teacher gave me that changed my life, and that I continue to use every single day. This is a simple but powerful combination of the two most important and vital practices in this book—welcoming and staying as Aware-ness. My teacher says that while you stay as Awareness, the body is an automatic self-cleaning mechanism. What that means is that while you stay or rest as Awareness, the trapped energy from every negative emotion is unwinding automatically and being released from your body by itself! You can sometimes feel the energy unwinding around the area of your chest.

Step 1. Welcome Anything Negative

Open your heart and welcome any negative reactions, negative feelings, negative sensations, negative thoughts or problems, in the moment they appear.

Step 2. Stay as Awareness

Stay as Awareness by keeping your attention wide like the lens on a camera, so it's not focused on any detail.

Because Awareness is naturally welcoming, you will find after doing the Super Practice for a while that the two steps merge into one. In the moment you welcome, you'll find that Awareness is instantaneously present.

Since doing this practice, I've noticed that negative emotions and reactions have become much weaker and evaporate quickly. I even reached a point where I loved a negative emotion or reaction to come up, because it not only reminded me to welcome it and stay as Awareness, but it felt *so good* when it dissolved.

I use the same practice when a negative situation, circumstance, or problem appears. I open my attention, open my heart, and welcome the negative feeling about the situation, and then I stay as Awareness the best I can. (A way to stay as Awareness that I have found to be invaluable is to love Awareness. Simply by loving Awareness you are giving your full attention to it.) I find that the negative situation changes very soon after I do this practice. It actually must change, because our resistance is what holds a negative situation to us!

"In the state of that awareness, all suffering ceases."
Jan Frazier, from When Fear Falls Away

A few years ago, I went through an event that would be considered by most people intensely scary and stressful. However, due to welcoming and staying as Awareness, the event didn't affect me the way it would have before I knew these practices.

Wildfires were threatening to destroy the community I live in. I was evacuated from my house, yet felt a peaceful state of calm about the safety of my home. I felt calm because I was fine with whatever happened. I had evacuated, and if I had lost my house, I absolutely knew it would be for the best, and that life needed to take me in a different direction. The fire was out of control for many weeks, destroying everything in its path. Eventually it loomed closer to my home and was burning houses in the road where I live. But I felt no fear, and no attachment to any outcome. I knew that I would remain happy no matter what happened. With no resistance to any outcome, my house remained safe. I had welcomed the situation, and I have no doubt that the peace and calm I felt through those fires was due to the welcoming I had practiced in the past.

"I've realized how much misery comes of resisting the present facts, or of living in the past or the future. I don't think I realized how much pain I was in before. It's like I was hitting myself on the shin with a hammer for fifty years, and then the hammer fell out of my hand."

Jan Frazier, from Opening the Door

To be free of negative emotions is worth every second that you put into it. I have been feeling good most of the time since I discovered The Secret in 2004, but these days I exist mostly in a state of gentle happiness due to the knowledge and practices I'm sharing with you in this book.

Can you imagine living a single day without any negative emotion affecting you whatsoever, let alone living a month that way, or a year? If you didn't have negative emotions, you wouldn't have negative thoughts to contradict what you want, and you would become a magnet for anything and everything you want! When you experience this for yourself, then you'll know that this is the true joy of living.

CHAPTER 7 *Summary*

- *Happiness is your natural state of being, so if you don't feel happiness right now, then you have a negative feeling that is stopping that happiness from being present.*

- *Be aware of a negative feeling without resisting it, expressing it, or judging it in any way, and see that it's just a feeling.*

- *The energy behind a negative feeling will naturally release when you allow the feeling to be present. It's an automatic process.*

- *Welcoming is a practice that eradicates negative feelings. Welcoming is the opposite of resisting. Welcoming says to a negative feeling, "Yes, you are welcome here."*

- *In the beginning it can be helpful if, when you open your attention, you also open your arms out to the sides of your body. You can consciously open your heart too.*

- *Use the welcoming process for anything that makes you feel bad, any negative thoughts or stories, negative feelings, painful sensations or memories, and limiting beliefs.*

- *When you have allowed a bad feeling to be present and you haven't suppressed it, that feeling will never be as strong in you again.*

- *Every negative feeling is there to direct you back home to who you are. They alert you to the fact that you're believing stories that are not true, so you can welcome those feelings and live your life as the magnificent Awareness that you truly are.*

- *A negative emotion only arises when you're ready to be free of it.*

- *When you release your negative feelings around a subject you feel strongly about, you are releasing all the energy you have focused on it and are dis-* empowering *the circumstances surrounding the subject.*

- *When we welcome a suppressed feeling evoked from a memory, all the hundreds and thousands of thoughts attached to that memory will be released with the feeling.*

- *The lightness, the happiness, and the "high" you feel as you release the feelings attached to painful memories cannot be described.*

- *The Super Practice*
  Step 1. Welcome anything negative.
  Step 2. Stay as Awareness (loving Awareness is one way to stay as Awareness).

CHAPTER 8

No More
Suffering

"Here's the bottom line: suffering is optional."
Byron Katie, from A Mind at Home with Itself

You are not meant to suffer. And when you're living as your true self, Awareness, you will never suffer. It can be hard to imagine a life without suffering, but most assuredly it can be your life, right now.

"There is pain in the physical, but suffering is of the mind."
Anthony de Mello, S.J.

"Your higher self does not suffer. Your familiar self can hardly figure out how not to suffer."
Jan Frazier, from The Freedom of Being

Suffering is caused by believing negative thoughts. So, suffering is self-imposed.

"I discovered that when I believed my thoughts, I suffered, but that when I didn't believe them, I didn't suffer, and that this is true for every human being. Freedom is as simple as that."
Byron Katie, from A Thousand Names for Joy

"Whenever you are suffering, your suffering is contained in a single thought: 'I don't like this.' In other words, we allow a single, flimsy, insubstantial thought to spoil our happiness."
Rupert Spira, from the talk, "Suffering Is Contained in a Single Thought"

Our mind tends to respond to the circumstances of life with No, No, No, while Awareness always responds with Yes, Yes, Yes, to everything.

"Awareness even says 'yes' to 'no'!"
My teacher

Saying "No" holds what you don't want to you. Saying "Yes" to what you don't want releases your resistance, allowing what you don't want to change. It's counterintuitive, but it's how it works. When you say, "No, I don't want this," you're resisting, and as you've come to understand, whatever you resist persists.

"If you abide in this state of acceptance, you create no more negativity, no more suffering, no more unhappiness. You then live in a state of nonresistance, a state of grace and lightness, free of struggle."
Eckhart Tolle, from The Power of Now

"I am a lover of what is, not because I'm a spiritual person, but because it hurts when I argue with reality."
Byron Katie, from Loving What Is

"If you were to altogether let go of resistance this moment, never to start it up again, by that single gesture, you'd liberate yourself from an enormous burden of suffering."
Jan Frazier, from The Freedom of Being

If we don't resist what has happened, there's no conflict, and the energy of the situation passes. Without our resistance to something, it can't stay in our life. On the other hand, if we resist what's happened, we'll hold the situation to us, and we'll continue to suffer. The wonderful teacher Sailor Bob Adamson says to just allow experiences to come and go without judging them.

"It is only the grasping, the hanging on, or the resisting and pushing away that creates the bind of psychological suffering."
Peter Lawry, from the talk "No Separation"

"Most people go to their graves believing suffering is unavoidable. How sad that is. If you turn from the possibility that it could be otherwise, you will suffer needlessly until the day you die. But here is something: the end of suffering would be the least of the benefits, if you became free. The real miracle is not the profound undoing of anguish, but the riches that would flood the freed-up 'space.'"
Jan Frazier, from When Fear Falls Away

An Instant End To Suffering

What I'm about to share with you may not be the easiest thing to grasp, but if you can get it, it will take you out of suffering immediately. Our mind makes it feel like *we* are the one who is suffering, and of course if we unquestioningly believe our mind, our suffering is immense. But the truth is that you are the one that is *aware* of the suffering, rather than the one suffering. The one who is suffering is the idea you have of yourself that you've believed but is not who you really are.

"The end of suffering happens when you recognize that there is no one to suffer."
Hale Dwoskin

My teacher would say to ask yourself this question:

"Am I the one suffering, or am I the one that is aware of the suffering?"

If we can stop believing the mind's suggestion that we're the one suffering, the suffering will end immediately.

"Once the nature of the mind is understood, suffering can't exist."
Byron Katie, from A Mind at Home with Itself

"Awareness opens the door, dissolves all the beliefs and opinions and ideas that are in the way of and covering up your natural state of happiness."
Anthony de Mello, S.J.

"It's no wonder that when the machinery of suffering has fallen apart, and the mind has grown quiet, the feeling is that you've come home. Home has found you—which is often the impression, since you hadn't necessarily been trying to find your way there, not consciously anyhow. Or maybe you had been, but now you see you'd been looking in the wrong places."

Jan Frazier, from The Great Sweetening: Life After Thought

There is one belief in particular that's the root cause of all the suffering in the world. It's the belief that we're a separate person. With thought, your mind convinces you that you are just a person, and that you are vulnerable to an entire world of things that could go wrong. If you believe the mind's story of separateness, you will be completely under the control of your mind. Your mind will send a constant feed of fearful thoughts that you are vulnerable, bad things can happen to you, and that you and your life are limited. Sadly, this will become your life if you believe it to be true. But the truth is the very opposite of this. We are not separate. There is the *appearance* that we're a separate person, and we're having the *experience* of being a separate person, but for a magnificent life filled with lasting happiness, stay aware of the truth that you are infinite, eternal, Consciousness-Awareness, and that there is only One of us.

The End of Problems

We believe we have a problem when something has gone differently from what we expected it to, or when we feel something has gone "wrong." Our mind's immediate response to a problem is: "I don't want this!" Yet:

"Problems exist only in the human mind."
Anthony de Mello, S.J., from Awareness: Conversations with the Masters

"Problems are not real. Problems are only imagined. There are no problems. It's impossible. What you are is free of problems. Problems are manufactured—every single one of them."
My teacher

"All problems are based on memory; in this moment, there are no problems."
Hale Dwoskin

"If there were no human mind, there would be no problems. All problems exist in the human mind. All problems are created by the mind."
Anthony de Mello, S.J., from Rediscovering Life

The truth is that problems are just another story created by the thoughts of our mind. It's the mind interpreting life by telling a story about something that's happened and turning it into a problem. To experience a problem-free life, instead of believing your mind, use the power of your Awareness to become *aware* of your mind.

When you're living more and more as Awareness, then you will see clearly that problems are imagined limitations. How can the Infinite Awareness that you are have a single problem?

"It's as if you put your hand in a fire and say, 'Ouch, it's hot! My hand is burning! Boy, do I have a problem!' And then you put your hand back in the fire, and so on, and so on, until one day you see that you are doing it and you stop. If you have a problem, you're putting your hand into a problem and yelling, 'It hurts!' and acting as though you're not putting your hand in it. You act as though you are not doing it. But you are."

Lester Levenson, from Happiness Is Free, *volumes 1–5*

"All problems come from the ego. You're free when you don't give validity to any problems."

My teacher

The difficulty is that when you *believe* you have a problem you will most definitely *experience* having a problem. But if you can be aware that it's really the mind and its thoughts telling another negative story, you allow any supposed problem to dissolve and disappear because your belief is not holding it to you or the world anymore.

"Anyone who says, 'I have trouble,' has it in his mind. That is the only place where it is, because you can't see or conceive of anything anywhere else but in your mind. Whatever you look at, whatever you hear, whatever you sense, is in and through your mind. That is where everything is."

Lester Levenson, from Happiness Is Free, *volumes 1–5*

"I'm going to tell you something very powerful. There is not a problem anywhere at any time. There is only a lack of love."

My teacher

When you don't resist anything, when you accept everything just the way that it is, this is love. Where love exists, no problem can exist. It's the reason why no problem can touch who you really are, because you are pure love. It is a love that is so pure our minds can't conceive of it. It is completely welcoming, accepting, all allowing, and totally unattached. It's the kind of love demonstrated by the remarkable enlightened beings like Buddha, Jesus Christ, Lao Tzu, Krishna, and so many more. And this pure love that you are has no problems ever.

But from the perspective of a limited person, problems do seem real. Our mind has the opposite reaction to Infinite Awareness, and it resists and denies the way something is rather than accepting and allowing it.

"Life is a series of natural and spontaneous changes. Don't resist them—that only creates sorrow. Let reality be reality. Let things flow naturally forward in whatever way they like."
Lao Tzu

"When there is no emotional investment in trying to force things to be the way we want them, then they are free to move and resolve themselves."
Kalyani Lawry

From using the principles of *The Secret* I've found that when I'm happy, there are barely any problems in my life. That's because from the place of happiness problems either don't appear, or they're so small that they don't have the ability to disturb my happiness. When I'm happy, problems look like anthills compared to when I've been in despair and the smallest problem appears to be mountainous. So doesn't it make sense that from the ultimate level of happiness, where we know who we are, there are zero problems?

"There's no end to problems in the world. If you try to find the end you go on and on forever and ever solving problems in the world and you will always find more and more. As long as you are conscious of problems they exist. Only when you discover the real you, will you discover an end to problems."

Lester Levenson, from Happiness Is Free, *volumes 1–5*

How To Be Free of Problems Forever

"You can be free from everything. Do you want to give a problem your attention by changing it, fixing it, or trying to figure it out, or do you want to be free of it?"

My teacher

When I shared with my teacher what I thought was a big problem, she said the following words to me. You could not have clearer words than these:

"Stop focusing into the problem. Stop wanting it to be more or less. Stop wanting it to go. Stop wanting to change it. Stop wanting to figure it out. Stop wanting to control it. It will naturally collapse when you decide to be Awareness. Everything that is not love collapses in the face of love. Everything that is not real collapses in the face of Awareness."

My teacher

As *The Secret* explained, when we give our attention to something, we energize it, so when we give our attention to a problem, we energize the problem and it gets bigger. Trying to fix a problem, trying to solve it, control it, or eradicate it, means we are giving our attention to the problem! When we shift our attention away from the problem, the problem disappears because all the energy has been removed from it. It has to collapse. It's like taking the oxygen out of a fire—the fire will go out.

"Now, trying to get rid of a problem is holding on to it. Anything we try to get rid of, we're holding in mind and therefore sustaining that problem. So, the only way to correct a problem is to let go of it. See not the problem. See only what you want."
Lester Levenson, from Will Power *audio*

And once you have taken your attention off any problem, then you can use your mind to create what you want, by focusing your mind and your thoughts on what you want.

"Energy flows where attention goes."
Michael Bernard Beckwith, from The Secret

We give our attention to what we don't want, expecting that will change it, when the opposite is true. We have to remove our attention to allow a problem to dissolve. I heard somebody once say that problems are like an unwelcome guest; if you don't give a guest any attention, they will leave!

Use the power of your Awareness to be aware of your mind's negative thoughts and stories, thereby dissolving them, and you will be free of all problems and suffering. It's simply another example of the joy and bliss that is yours when you stay as the Awareness that you are.

"This is a gently unfolding miracle. Be patient. All your life, you've been doing it the other way, believing yourself to be at the mercy of life. Don't expect the whole thing to undo itself all at once."
Jan Frazier, from The Freedom of Being

CHAPTER 8 *Summary*

- *You are not meant to suffer. And when you're living as your true self, Awareness, you will never suffer.*

- *Suffering is caused by believing negative thoughts. So, suffering is self-imposed.*

- *If we resist what's happened, we'll hold the situation to us, and we'll continue to suffer.*

- *Ask yourself this question: "Am I the one suffering, or am I the one that is aware of the suffering?" The truth is that you are the one that is aware of the suffering, rather than the one suffering.*

- *There is one belief in particular that's the root cause of all the suffering in the world. It's the belief that we're a separate person.*

- *Problems exist only in the human mind. Problems are not real. Problems are only imagined.*

- *To experience a problem-free life, instead of believing your mind, use the power of your Awareness to become aware of your mind.*

- *When we give our attention to a problem, we energize the problem and it gets bigger. When we shift our attention away from the problem, the problem disappears because all the energy has been removed from it.*

- *Once you have taken your attention off any problem, then you can use your mind to create what you want, by focusing your mind and your thoughts on what you want.*

- *Use the power of your Awareness to be aware of your mind's negative thoughts and stories, thereby dissolving them, and you will be free of all problems and suffering.*

DISSOLVING
LIMITING BELIEFS

"All beliefs are imagined limitations."
My teacher

What *is* a belief? A belief is just a thought that we think over and over again—until we believe it. All beliefs are limited because they come from the mind. Let's look at an example: the belief that says something is "too good to be true." We first hear it said by others, then we begin having the thought ourselves, after a while we believe it's true, and then we start to see evidence of it in the world. The very moment we believe it is true it becomes a belief stored in our subconscious mind, and from that moment on that belief operates as an automatic program in our subconscious, and it must project itself in the world and continue to prove itself to be true in our life.

"A thought is harmless until we believe it."
Byron Katie

"It is not what the ego says, it is how much it is believed."
Mooji

Beliefs also throw up other thoughts based on the belief, and the thoughts play like recordings. With the belief "something is too good to be true," the subconscious mind will play thoughts like: "When I feel this happy, I feel like something bad is going to happen." "Make the most of it, this isn't going to last." "Something bad always follows something good." "I'm feeling nervous because good things don't usually happen to me." "If something feels too good to be true, you can bet it is." These thoughts are probably familiar to you, which proves they are just recordings from the mind and they're not unique to you.

My teacher said, imagine if you answered the phone and there was a recording on the other end saying: "This is a recorded message. Transfer all your money into this bank account right now so we can keep it safe." Would you do it? Would you believe the recording? No, of course you wouldn't believe it. But then why believe the recordings of the mind?

Your Beliefs Cause Your Experience

"We project our thoughts and beliefs and they return to us as our experience."
David Bingham

You must experience whatever you believe, so it matters a great deal what your beliefs are. Beliefs have what could be described as atomic power, because they will continually project themselves into your life and make themselves true. It doesn't matter that they're false; if you've planted a belief in the subconscious it will bear fruit.

For example, you can't have the belief that the only way you can receive more money is through working harder and longer hours, and then receive cash windfalls from multiple places you never expected. Your belief prevents money coming in from other sources. This is how much we limit ourselves through our beliefs. When you have a belief about a person, circumstance, or situation, you must experience it. Thoughts have no power of their own without the energy of your belief behind them.

"There is only one cause of unhappiness: the false beliefs you have in your head, beliefs so widespread, so commonly held, that it never occurs to you to question them."
Anthony de Mello, S.J., from The Way to Love

"Unhappiness is caused only by false beliefs about what Life really is."
Peter Dziuban, from Simply Notice

We can also become very attached to our beliefs, even when they cause us real stress and suffering and imprison us in misery. Our beliefs can keep us poor, make us sick, fill us with fear, and damage or destroy our relationships. They are really nothing to treasure or hold on to.

Whatever circumstances are appearing in your life currently are being generated by your belief system in your subconscious mind.

"By changing the beliefs we are holding, we can amend the experiences we are having."
David Bingham

"Many of our ideas and beliefs about ourselves and the world are so deeply ingrained that we are unaware that they are beliefs and take them, without questioning, for the absolute truth."
Rupert Spira, from The Transparency of Things

From the late Dr. David R. Hawkins:

"It is often beneficial to look at some commonly held beliefs and let go of them right in the beginning such as:

1. We only deserve things through hard work, struggle, sacrifice, and effort.

2. Suffering is beneficial and good for us.

3. We don't get anything for nothing.

4. Things that are very simple aren't worth much."
Dr. David R. Hawkins, from Letting Go

The great sages urge us to question everything. Through questioning, we can discover our limiting beliefs that are covering up the truth about us and the truth behind the world.

"Nothing you believe is true. Knowing this is freedom."
Byron Katie

We have stockpiled beliefs in our subconscious since we were a small child and were able to comprehend something of what was being communicated to us by adults. Beliefs are formed when we accept a particular thought as true, whether that's something we've read or heard on television, or when we accept an idea that others have told us. One way or another, all of our beliefs have come from others, whether from parents, family, friends, teachers, or society. In the moment we believe what someone else tells us, bingo, into the subconscious goes the belief, where it will play out in our life!

For example, if a person believes, "I have trouble losing weight and keeping it off," that belief will prevent weight from staying off no matter what the person does.

Over time, beliefs become more entrenched in the subconscious as we add more and more thoughts to them, like: "It must be my metabolism that makes it so difficult for me to lose weight." "I've tried heaps of diets, but I can't seem to keep the weight off." "It takes me ages to lose the weight, and in no time I put it back on." "Being overweight runs in my family."

"The subconscious mind is running us—making us the victims of habit."
Lester Levenson, from Happiness Is Free, *volumes 1–5*

The great news is that because beliefs are simply made up of flimsy thoughts, they can be eradicated quite easily once you become aware of them. While beliefs remain stored in the subconscious mind, they will automatically continue to play out in your life. But the moment you become truly aware of one of your beliefs, the belief is dismantled. Just like when all negative feelings are released, when all subconscious beliefs become conscious, the result is that you permanently remain as Awareness. Actually, when you eradicate one, you simultaneously eradicate the other. I take a double-pronged approach, and release both beliefs and negative feelings whenever they appear.

Exposing your limiting beliefs takes you rapidly to lasting happiness and complete freedom. In the process, your worldly life dramatically improves in each and every area, because it's no longer limited by beliefs. If there's something you think you can't be, do, or have, that's a limiting belief. Imagine your life without any limitations!

Dissolving Beliefs

You dissolve beliefs with Awareness—by becoming consciously aware of them. The moment you are *aware* a belief is not true, most of it collapses and dissolves. If you continue to bring the belief up into your thinking mind, reminding yourself that it's just a belief and isn't true, under that scrutiny the rest of the belief will totally dissolve. This is the infinite power of Awareness.

It can be a bit tricky to spot your beliefs, for the very reason that you believe they're the truth rather than a belief! However, once you become aware of a belief the dissolution begins, and what's left of the belief will collapse through the continued awareness of it.

You can even reach a point where you can't remember what you used to believe, because the belief has truly vanished. Beliefs and memories both consist of thought, and they're stored in our subconscious mind, so if a belief is erased, all the thoughts attached to the belief will also be gone, including the thoughts making up the memory of it.

"Surrender everything you believe. You have to, sooner or later. You cannot take your belief systems with you when you pass away so why not surrender them now? Surrender your beliefs from moment to moment. Discover the joy of living without attachment to any belief system. The attachment to beliefs such as, 'Happiness requires effort' or 'It is necessary to suffer in order to be happy' is very deep."
Francis Lucille, from The Perfume of Silence

Every belief you become aware of and consequently dissolve will propel your life to heights of freedom, abundance, lightness, and joy you never could have imagined. Take those beliefs out, one by one, and set yourself free! Awareness doesn't have any beliefs because Awareness *knows* everything.

"In fact, belief systems are nothing. They are quite easy to let go of. They are just paper tigers! It is better to let them go right now and live happily forever after."
Francis Lucille, from The Perfume of Silence

You can give the subconscious mind an instruction to highlight your beliefs for you, so you can become more aware of them. Instruct your subconscious with words like these: "Show me my beliefs clearly one by one, so I become aware of each and every one of them." Then stay very aware so you notice them when they appear.

Be very aware when you hear yourself say, "I believe" or "I don't believe," because immediately following those words is a belief. Be very aware when you hear yourself say, "I think" or "I don't think," because most likely what will follow that will also reveal a belief.

When you see that a belief is really just a mental story that you've bought into, the belief not only dissolves but also takes with it the thousands upon thousands of thoughts attached to that belief—all of which have been buried in the subconscious mind. Beliefs are not only made of thought, they constantly draw to themselves new thoughts that support the belief, and they will keep accumulating thoughts for as long as we retain the belief.

A belief can be held for years, decades, or a lifetime, which explains why, with thousands of thoughts attached to one belief, so many of us feel heavy and burdened. We don't realize that it's our beliefs that make our life so heavy, and make us feel older, and that it's our beliefs that hold us back from having the life we deserve. Just imagine, for example, how many thoughts you would have attached to the belief that you are just a person separate from everyone else. Now imagine the enormous sense of relief, lightness, and spaciousness you would feel when a belief that size dissolves. You will know the feeling for yourself when you experience it!

"Be like a tree and let the dead leaves drop."
Rumi

Reactions: Beliefs in Disguise

"Reactions are unconscious beliefs."
Peter Dziuban, from Simply Notice *audiobook*

Another way to expose beliefs is through becoming aware of your reactions. When we react to something, it's because we have a belief buried within us that caused the reaction. Reactions are actually beliefs in disguise. For example: We receive our electricity bill, which is much larger than we expected. We react negatively. The belief that caused the reaction is a belief in a lack of money, but like all beliefs, it's only true in our life *because* we believe it.

All you have to do when you notice yourself reacting is become aware of the reaction. When you're aware of the reaction, you take the power out of it because your Awareness is the power that dissolves every bit of negativity and disharmony.

"When you react you're identifying; when you react you're making something personal. Instead, just notice the reaction."
My teacher

Remember that it's the mind that reacts to things, not you. It's the mind that identifies with things and makes things personal, because it's coming from the perspective of a person. When you become aware of your reactions—by just noticing them in the moment—you not only take the power out of your mind to react, you also expose the belief that is hiding underneath the reaction, and once exposed it will dissolve.

"If there's a behavior, tendency or habit you wish to be free of, notice there is already a natural awareness of it. If you really see this, if you observe it with detachment, you will instantly feel out of its grip and free from further identifying with it. This is very significant."
Mooji

Awareness dissolves everything that is not true. As each belief dissolves, one by one, you will feel the difference in your body; you will feel lighter. You will feel the difference in your mental health; you will feel happier. You will see the difference in your life; your life will become truly effortless and miraculous. Whatever you need, whatever you want, will seem to just fall into your hands.

I would like to share another part of the amazing Lester Levenson's story. If you recall, Lester became enlightened in three months and at the same time cured his body of multiple diseases. Before this, Lester had developed severe heart problems at just forty years old, and was given a death sentence by his doctor. The doctor said that Lester could die any day, and there was nothing they could do. Lester went home, and for the first few days was terrified of dying. Then he decided that if he was going to die, he would at least reflect back on his life and work out why he had rarely been happy. This began the process whereby Lester removed every belief and suppressed negative emotion in his body in just three months. With all the negativity gone from his body, the heart condition spontaneously resolved itself, and Lester lived for another forty years in perfect health and continuous joy. More importantly, with the removal of all of his beliefs and suppressed emotions, Lester discovered who he really was.

And now you know how he did it.

CHAPTER 9 *Summary*

- *A belief is just a thought that we think over and over again—until we believe it. All beliefs are limited because they come from the mind.*

- *A belief is stored in our subconscious mind where it operates as an automatic program.*

- *Beliefs will continually project themselves into your life and make themselves true.*

- *Whatever circumstances are appearing in your life currently are being generated by your belief system.*

- *Be very aware when you hear yourself say, "I believe" or "I don't believe," because immediately following those words is a belief.*

- *Be very aware when you hear yourself say, "I think" or "I don't think," because most likely what will follow that will also reveal a belief.*

- *Question everything. Through questioning, we can discover limiting beliefs we're holding on to that are obscuring the truth.*

- *While beliefs remain stored in the subconscious mind, they will automatically continue to play out in your life. But the moment you become truly aware of a belief you hold, the belief is dismantled.*

- *Every belief you become aware of and consequently dissolve will propel your life to heights of freedom, abundance, lightness, and joy.*

- *You can give the subconscious mind an instruction to highlight your beliefs for you, so you can become more aware of them: "Show me my beliefs clearly one by one, so I become aware of each and every one of them."*

- *When a belief dissolves, it also takes with it the thousands upon thousands of thoughts attached to that belief, which have also been buried in the subconscious mind.*

- *We don't realize that it's our beliefs that make our life so heavy, and make us feel older, and that it's our beliefs that hold us back from having the life we deserve.*

- *To expose your beliefs, be aware of your reactions. Reactions are actually beliefs in disguise.*

- *All you have to do when you notice yourself reacting is become aware of the reaction. When you're aware of the reaction, you take the power out of it.*

CHAPTER 10

EVERLASTING
HAPPINESS

"I am living in the eternally happy present. It is not a mundane happiness, which becomes boring after a while so that you welcome a little difficulty just for a change. The joy that has come upon me is a thousand million times more intoxicating—ever-changing, ever-new. In that consciousness you feel all the happiness in the world passing through you."

Paramahansa Yogananda

You *are* happiness. It is your true nature! Happiness is not something that will happen once you've received something you want, when you feel better, get through something challenging, or reach a particular goal. Happiness—a never-ending wellspring of happiness—is here right now inside you!

"One must realize the Self in order to open the store of unalloyed happiness."

Ramana Maharshi, from Be as You Are

"Don't expect to attain unalloyed peace and happiness from earthly life. This should be your new attitude: no matter what your experiences are, enjoy them in an objective way, as you would a movie. You have to find true peace and happiness within yourself."

Paramahansa Yogananda, from Man's Eternal Quest

"Happiness is our natural state. Happiness is the natural state of little children, to whom the kingdom belongs until they have been polluted and contaminated by society and culture. To acquire happiness, you don't have to do anything, because happiness cannot be acquired. Does anybody know why? Because we have it already. How can you acquire what you already have? Then why don't you experience it? You've got to drop illusions. You don't have to add anything in order to be happy; you've got to drop something. Life is easy, life is delightful. It's only hard on your illusions."
Anthony de Mello, S.J., from Awareness: Conversations with the Masters

I now live with an undercurrent of happiness that's with me all the time, which came from welcoming negative feelings and staying as Awareness. However, there have been several times when I have had a truly blissful happiness sweep over me that's beyond anything I've felt before. It seems to come out of nowhere. What I mean by that is there wasn't anything that caused it. When it appears, all negativity totally disappears. Any painful memories from my life are gone in that moment, as though they never really happened. This blissful happiness is instantly recognizable to me as the happiness of our true nature. It can't be compared to the happiness we feel from getting something we want. This is a level of happiness that is above and beyond anything else I've ever felt.

I'm hoping, in sharing this with you, that you can open yourself to the possibility of experiencing it, too. Once you've felt your natural state of happiness, from then on you will only want to live your life in that state.

"I found a joy within me that has never disappeared, not for a single moment. That joy is in everyone, always."
Byron Katie, from A Thousand Names for Joy

This happiness is like the feeling of falling in love, whether it's falling in love with a partner or a mother falling in love with her new baby. You know that blissful feeling of being head over heels, totally and completely in love? You never want the feeling to end. The reason why we experience such a blissful feeling when we fall in love is because we lose "ourselves" in the other person, and when we lose the ego mind, Awareness is instantly present in the foreground, radiantly joyful, and blissfully happy.

"Everyone is seeking the exact same thing in his every act. The world calls it the ultimate happiness. We call it the 'I' that I am. Discover yourself and you discover the greatest happiness and you get the greatest contentment."
Lester Levenson

"Quite simply put, happiness is you being your Self. Not the limited self that you pretend to be most of the time, but the unlimited Self that you are and have always been. This is the Self that is always effortlessly present before, during, and after everything else that appears in your experience. You are the radiant yet changeless background that allows for everything else to exist."
Hale Dwoskin, from Happiness Is Free

"To find Truth or Happiness you have to go within—you have to see the Oneness, you have to see the Universe as it really is, as nothing but your consciousness, which is nothing but your Self. Now this is difficult to describe—it is something that must be experienced. Only when someone experiences it does one know. It cannot be picked up from listening to anyone. Books and teachers can only point the direction. It is up to us to take it. That's one of the nice things about the path. There's nothing to be believed, everything must be experienced and proved by each person to his own satisfaction before it's accepted."

Lester Levenson, from Happiness Is Free, *volumes 1–5*

Awareness Equals Happiness

You are not a person who is happy—you are happiness itself. Your true nature, Awareness, *is* happiness. There's no other happiness but the happiness of your true nature. The happiness you have felt at any time in your life *is* the happiness of Awareness! During those times when you felt happy, you were getting a tiny glimpse of the magnificence that you are.

"Understand that a moment of happiness comes from grace, and this moment of happiness is teaching us that happiness is not in an object. We have to know that we are this happiness in the moment. The object is almost irrelevant. The object is part of the dream, but the happiness is real."

Francis Lucille, from The Perfume of Silence

And when you are happy, life will go your way. There's nothing better for your life circumstances than you feeling happy. When you are happy, problems tend to solve themselves, and things fall into place easily, without any effort from you. When you're happy, it's as though the entire Universe is conspiring on your behalf and presenting whatever you need in the moment you need it. The happier you are, the more effortless is your life. The more unhappy you are, the more effort it will take for everything you do.

"The more ego motivated you are, the more difficult it is to accomplish something, the less is the harmony and the greater is the misery."
Lester Levenson, from Happiness Is Free, *volumes 1–5*

There's No Happiness in the World

"Some of us are seeking Happiness where it is and as a result becoming happier. And others are seeking it blindly in the world where it is not and are becoming more frustrated."
Lester Levenson, from Happiness Is Free, *volumes 1–5*

When we seek happiness in the world, our happiness is fleeting. No matter how many things we acquire, or how many experiences we have, the happiness from material things or experiences is bound to come and go. And then we're back seeking happiness through the next material thing or experience. Lasting happiness, which we've convinced ourselves is in the world, simply isn't there.

"Yet only when we go within, do we discover that all happiness is there. The only place where we can feel happiness is right within ourselves. That is exactly where it is. Every time we attribute this happiness to something external, to a person or a thing external, we get more pain with it than we do pleasure."
Lester Levenson, from Happiness Is Free, *volumes 1–5*

"We don't have to wait for the right circumstances to be happy."
Rupert Spira

Every person who has ever lived or is currently living has been driven by the same singular purpose—the desire for happiness. Everything we do, everything we don't do, everything we strive for, design, plot against, live for, wish for, and dream of is because we think we will be happier from the having of it or not having of it. Wanting happiness is the single motivating factor behind every decision each person makes—and it's estimated we make 35,000 decisions a day! Yet all of the plotting, planning, actions, sweat, tears, and decision-making is not taking us any closer to the happiness we vainly seek in the world. All along, the happiness we seek has been right here within us.

"And what is the way out? Not looking to the world for happiness, but looking to the place where happiness is, right within us, within our own consciousness."
Lester Levenson, from Happiness Is Free, *volumes 1–5*

I'll Be Happy When . . .

When we believe happiness comes from outside of us, we can easily fall into a habit of putting our happiness on hold until conditions are right. Have you ever thought or said, "I'll be happy when . . ." and finished the sentence with some event in the future? "I'll be happy when exams are over and I graduate," "I'll be happy when I get a new car," "I'll be happy when I find a partner," "I'll be happy when I'm married," "I'll be happy when I have more money," "I'll be happy when I've become successful," "I'll be happy when I'm on vacation," "I'll be happy when I've lost weight," "I'll be happy when we have a baby," "I'll be happy when my business is up and running," "I'll be happy when my health is improved and I feel better," and the list goes on.

We put our happiness on hold when we believe that happiness comes from external things. We wait for something or someone to make us happy, but it's impossible to have lasting happiness from external things; it will never happen, no matter how long we wait.

Perhaps if you have lived long enough, been successful enough, and had lots of wonderful life experiences, you have already discovered that happiness can't be found in the world. You especially may have seen the truth of this if a really big dream has come true for you. We convince ourselves that when our biggest dream comes true—like achieving great success, acquiring wealth, finding our perfect partner, or having children—we will finally be truly happy.

But when a huge dream does come true, while it's wonderful and exciting, we discover that the lasting happiness we thought we would have is almost as fleeting as it has been with everything else. We may finally realize through our own bitter experience that happiness doesn't come from the external world. It can be a pretty deflating moment for some, because often a conclusion is reached that lasting happiness is a fantasy and will never happen.

But lasting happiness is not a fantasy. It is the truth of your very being, and it is your very nature. After all of our needless searching, it's a momentous discovery when you finally see that the happiness you seek is right now within your very own self! When you can see the truth of it, lasting happiness will be within your grasp, because you'll never look in vain to other people or the world for your happiness again.

"When you see that, it makes the path very direct. You stop chasing the rainbow, and you go for the happiness where you know it is—right within you."
Lester Levenson, from Happiness Is Free, volumes 1–5

Imagine it. Billions of people over many thousands of years have been desperately searching for happiness every day of their lives. Searching for it as if it could be found in all kinds of worldly places. And all along there's only one place where it can be found—in our true nature, Awareness. The whole setup is like one big cosmic joke, which is perhaps why Buddha laughed so hard under the Bodhi tree when, after a sixteen-year worldly search, he finally discovered that the truth was within him. If you think about it, history has shown that not many of us ever thought to look for happiness inside us.

Yet we have all been given many signposts in our lives, often through bitter experience, that showed us happiness doesn't come from the world. Every time happiness came and went in your life, it was another signpost directing you to turn away from the world and look within.

Now we can look for happiness where it is, instead of where it isn't. You can stop looking to your partner or children for lasting happiness. You can stop looking to your job, a new home, clothes, vacation, or a car for lasting happiness. None of those things can possibly make you permanently happy because they're always changing. Not to mention that your personality is always changing; what you like today, you don't like tomorrow. Your happiness is within the *real*, unchanging you, Awareness. No one can give it to you.

Certainly, we can enjoy all the wonderful things that we want to be, do, or have in the world, but we can enjoy those things with the full knowledge that the only place to find real, permanent happiness is within us.

"You do not acquire happiness. Your very nature is happiness. Bliss is not newly earned. All that is done is to remove unhappiness."
Ramana Maharshi

Your thoughts determine how you're feeling, so if you're not happy, it's because you're thinking about something you don't want. Your mind can only function in the past or the future, so either you're thinking of something in the past that's making you unhappy or you're thinking of something in the future that's making you unhappy.

"Thoughts smother the capacity to be happy."
Lester Levenson, from Happiness Is Free, *volumes 1–5*

Standing between you and permanent happiness and who you really are is one thought. Whether it's a sad thought, a fearful thought, an angry thought, or a frustrating thought, in the end all of those thoughts are saying the same thing—"I don't want this"—in response to something that has happened. And because of believing that one thought, unhappiness descends upon you like a blanket, and covers the happiness that you truly are.

"Thought comes first, then feeling, then emotion (like tears). It always happens that way and often people first feel the emotion, and don't realize that there was a subtle thought first that created the feeling and then came the emotion."
Sailor Bob Adamson

"The only reason you're experiencing that you're unhappy is because you're identifying with an unhappy thought."
My teacher

"Life is simple. Everything happens *for* you, not *to* you. Everything happens at exactly the right moment, neither too soon nor too late. You don't have to like it . . . it's just easier if you do."
Byron Katie, from A Thousand Names for Joy

Hopefully you are starting to see the havoc that can be wreaked in your life when you believe your mind and its negative thoughts. Any time that I have had the opportunity to help someone with a difficulty or challenge they were facing, the reason for their suffering has always been because of believing their mind's negative thoughts. Any time that I have experienced any difficulty in my own life has also been because I believed my mind and its negative thoughts. So, if you can, when you feel pain or some hurt from a situation, let that hurtful feeling be a wake-up call telling you that right now you are believing negative thoughts that are not true. Once you stop believing your mind, you will start to notice that your mind is inclined to object to most things, masking your innate happiness.

"What's wrong with right now if you don't think about it?"
Sailor Bob Adamson, from A Sprinkling of Jewels

"The peace that you are seeking is already present. That peace is seemingly obscured because our attention is being diverted into thinking."
Kalyani Lawry

"We say *peace of mind*, but what we really want is *peace from mind*."
Seneca

With all of the mind's chatter, nonstop commentary, contradictory nature, and beating up on us, it's surprising that so many of us still believe our mind as though it is *the* authority in the world. You don't have to stop, still, or quiet your mind; you just have to stop believing it! When you stop believing it, it will automatically become quieter, and then happiness will arise in you like a tidal wave of bliss.

Resisting Happiness

As incredible as it is to hear, many of us resist being happy. We don't realize we're doing it because our resistance is coming from a suppressed belief. The belief could have been put there when we were children and we were told to curb our natural, free-spirited enthusiasm and joy. Did you ever hear things like: "Act your age," "Grow up," "Stop showing off," or "Calm down and be quiet"? If you did, you might have a belief that to get approval you have to be calm and quiet, because when you were running around excited and in joy, you got in trouble for being noisy. As a result, slowly over time we became accustomed to damping down and restraining our natural joy. But simply by realizing that we've been resisting happiness we break that belief and take most of the power out of it.

"We're naturally happy so if we're not experiencing happiness, we're resisting happiness."
My teacher

"If you were not actively engaged in making yourself miserable—you would be happy."
Anthony de Mello, S.J., from Rediscovering Life

We don't have to do anything to be happy. Instead, we need to stop doing what we're doing that's making us unhappy!

"It is not challenging to be happy. It is challenging to be unhappy. When you say that it is challenging to be happy, it suggests that happiness involves effort, constant vigilance, struggle. If we believe that happiness requires effort and struggle, it only perpetuates misery."
Francis Lucille, from The Perfume of Silence

"Can't you sense the underlying unlimited happiness of your being?"
My teacher

If our natural state is happiness, then imagine the enormous amount of energy it takes to be unhappy.

All over the world, resistance is the one thing that has robbed the majority of people's happiness. Rather than allowing things to be as they are, we resist what is happening or what has happened with the singular, repetitive thought of, "I don't want . . ." And then fill in the blank with the never-ending list of "don't wants."

"Nothing external can disturb us. We suffer only when we want things to be different from what they are."
Byron Katie, from Loving What Is

"Happiness is simply to allow everything to be exactly as it is from moment to moment."
Rupert Spira

If you can stop resisting what is happening in your life and the world, then blissful happiness is yours. Enlightenment is simply another word for blissful happiness. Enlightened is what you are already. Blissful happiness is what you are already. They're not something that only a select few can experience—they *are you*, and everyone else!

Attachment

"If you look carefully, you will see that there is one thing and only one thing that causes unhappiness. The name of that thing is attachment."
Anthony de Mello, S.J., from The Way to Love

Attachment comes when we hold on to something for fear of losing it because we believe that we can't be happy without it. Attachment is often mistaken for love, but attachment is not love. Love has no fear in it whatsoever. Love allows everything to be free, whether those things come or whether they go. Attachment masks itself as love, but attachment wants to grasp on to something for fear of losing it.

"The thing that is blind is not love but attachment. An attachment is the state of clinging that comes from the false belief that something or someone is necessary for your happiness."
Anthony de Mello, S.J., from The Way to Love

Imagine two people who have jobs in the same company. They both say they love their work and they're happy going to work every day.

Then one day they arrive at work, and they hear that staff is being cut that very day. Person A's body immediately fills with fear when he hears the news. "What will I do if I get cut? What if I can't get another job? I won't be able to pay my bills or my mortgage. I'll lose my home." All of these thoughts come from attachment to his job. You can recognize the fear in these thoughts.

Meanwhile, person B has a different perspective. He knows he will be happy no matter what happens. He knows that things in life are always changing, and everything happens for the best despite how it sometimes appears at the time. He knows from his own experience that when something unexpected happens, something better is coming. If for any reason his job gets cut, he knows he will find another job, and he knows it will work out to be even better. This is nonattachment.

Who do you think is the happier person? Who do you think has a better life?

"As a matter of fact, you have no idea of what happiness is until you've dropped attachment."
Anthony de Mello, S.J., from Rediscovering Life

"My life is a succession of events, just like yours. Only I am detached and see the passing show as a passing show, while you stick to things and move along with them."
Nisargadatta Maharaj, from I Am That: Talks with Sri Nisargadatta Maharaj

In the case of an attachment to a person, the attachment comes from a belief in a lack of love. You believe that this one person holds the key to your love and happiness, and without them your love and happiness will be gone. The belief justifies the attachment and puts you in extreme jeopardy, because everything is changing all the time, and no "body" is here forever.

"People need each other and think it is love. There's no hanging on to, or fencing in, of the other one when one loves."
Lester Levenson

Attachments run very deep. Often our attachments make up the identity of the person we think we are, and we feel that if we dropped our attachments, we would lose our identity. So, we cling to our attachments, when all along they rob us of our happiness and imprison us in misery.

When you believe there's a limited amount of something, you become attached to what you have. We can have attachments to our body, mind, the image we have of ourselves, our partner, children, parents, family, friends, pets, career, personal achievements, fame, skills, hobbies, religion, success, and material objects like our car or our house, as well as attachments to our opinions, beliefs, and points of view. You have probably seen people fiercely defending their beliefs in politics, religion, and a whole host of other subjects because of their deep attachment to their opinions.

"We are so married to our thoughts that we never even think of divorcing them. And, until we do, we will continue, blindly attached to physical bodies and, in the overall, having a miserable life."
Lester Levenson, from Happiness Is Free, *volumes 1–5*

Over the years our mind can become deeply attached to a myriad of fixed ideas. It's ironic that these ideas that we cling to actually bind us to being a limited person, make our life heavy, and stifle our natural happiness.

History has shown us that people can be so attached to their beliefs they will die rather than let go of them. For some people, their attachments to their beliefs are the only things that keep them going despite their misery.

"People don't want to be happy. To be happy they have to change their beliefs and ideas and they cling to them. They say, no way. We refuse to be happy unless our desires are fulfilled."
Anthony de Mello, S.J.

If you could empty yourself of all of your opinions and fixed ideas one by one, you would be enlightened, because when you're free of all judgment, you allow things to be just as they are. And then you would be in awe of the joy and happiness that would flood through your very being, not to mention how your life would naturally spiral upward in every area.

As I wrote in *The Secret*, Tenth Anniversary Edition, the fewer opinions you have, the fewer conclusions you come to, the fewer fixed ideas you hold to, the more bliss and joy will be yours.

What is actually attached is not *you*, but your mind! Attachments are a picnic for the mind because attachments strengthen the mind and keep us imprisoned in the belief that we're a limited, separate person, instead of the unlimited, blissfully happy Awareness that we really are. Because attachments come from your mind, you will feel a palpable fear when something the mind is attached to is threatened.

And the biggest attachment your mind has is its attachment to being an ego and an individual person. Even though the truth—that we are really the one Awareness—is so wondrous, still our mind clings to the idea of being a separate person.

There is no outcome to a life with attachment other than heartbreak and suffering, because nothing in this material world is lasting or permanent, including our bodies. Without you realizing it, your mind has traded your happiness for attachments.

Anthony de Mello summed up attachment beautifully in his interpretation of the Buddha's Four Noble Truths:

"The world is full of sorrow.
The root of sorrow is attachment desire.
The solution to a life without sorrow is the
dropping of attachment."
Anthony de Mello, S.J., from Rediscovering Life

You can desire and have whatever you want; the problem only comes when you're attached to those things.

Awareness Versus Attachment

You don't have to struggle to try to eliminate your attachments. You don't have to put a whole lot of effort into trying to change the way you feel. Attachment comes from identifying with the mind, and so to free yourself of attachments all you have to do is just stay as Awareness more and more, and all of your attachments will drop one by one! I cannot begin to tell you how incredible life is when you're not ruled by attachments. The love that you feel for everyone and everything is much deeper, and yet at the same time you don't feel an unbearable sadness when something ends or changes.

"This is my secret. I don't mind what happens."
J. Krishnamurti, from the second public talk, Ojai, 1977

Krishnamurti's words show us what it's like not to be attached to anything. His words are true nonattachment. And while I know it's possibly hard for you to believe that you could ever feel this way, that is only the mind telling you that. Remember, nonattachment is your true nature; nonattachment *is you*, Awareness.

Many years ago, my family and I had a beautiful house in the Australian countryside. My two children loved living in the country, and they loved that house. It was a magical life, but unfortunately interest rates climbed to over 18 percent, and despite taking on extra work and longer hours, in the end my husband and I could not pay our mortgage. We put ourselves through enormous sacrifice and suffering for three years trying to hold on to that house, and still we lost it. On the day we finally moved out, I thought about the misery we had put ourselves through, and I decided I would never get attached to another house again. When we suffer enough, we will change.

Since then, I have loved every house I've lived in—some I've loved and enjoyed more than any others before—but I've not been attached to any of them. While I was living in them, I enjoyed and appreciated them fully, without any fear of not having them one day. And when it was time to walk away from them, I was able to do so with only gratitude in my heart, and with no sadness whatsoever.

"Happiness occurs when we're not attached to any object, including the body, and material things."
Francis Lucille

We're here in the material world, and all things material must come to an end. If we're attached to something, it will guarantee suffering when it goes. But if you deeply love what is here now in your life—if you're truly grateful for what is here now, and if you appreciate it fully—you will never feel the same degree of pain when it goes.

I had a very close relationship with my mother through my childhood and adult years. She was more than my mother; I also considered her to be my best friend. I used to be terrified of her dying because I couldn't imagine living without her or having any kind of worthwhile life if she was no longer in it. After I discovered The Secret, I became filled with gratitude and appreciation for everything in my life, especially for my family and my mother. I appreciated every moment with her. I would tell her constantly about all the little things and big things she had done for me throughout my life that meant so much to me. I would tell her constantly how much I loved her. So, when my mother passed, I didn't suffer as I would have earlier in my life. Instead, I felt my love for my mother expand to be bigger than the Universe. And to this day, it has never changed.

You are love, and love is the stark opposite of attachment because love grants everything its freedom to come or go. Love is accepting and allowing of everything, no matter what happens.

"Love is what you are already. Love doesn't seek anything. It's already complete. It doesn't want, doesn't need, has no shoulds."
Byron Katie, from I Need Your Love—Is That True?

I can promise you that as your attachments drop, the love you will feel is so full and so big that you will feel as though the Universe can't hold it. All the things you were attached to will be replaced by this love that is omnipotent, omniscient, and omnipresent. Some call this love "God."

When people found themselves in the presence of Jesus, Buddha, Krishna, or any other fully enlightened being, any negativity within them dissolved immediately. That's how powerful pure, unconditional love is. It will dissolve all discord and negativity immediately. It will dissolve anything and everything that is not love. This all-powerful love is your true nature. It is you.

Begin with Happiness

"You need nothing to be happy. You need something to be sad."
Sri Poonja (Papaji)

"When we see that [awareness is present all the time], a transformation takes place in the body-mind. The body-mind is

struck by causeless joy and is set free from the belief that it has to work towards the acquisition of happiness. The happiness is not something that can be reached through effort, through suffering. How could we reach happiness through suffering? How could more suffering make us happy? We have to start from happiness. So often we have accepted more suffering in order to become happy."
Francis Lucille, from The Perfume of Silence

You can be happy in this very moment, no matter what is going on around you. Happiness is not something you have to look for or wait for, because it's here with you right now.

"We can have freedom and happiness now. We don't have to wait for it to arrive some far-off day in the future when we have worked hard enough to deserve it or when we have succeeded somehow in making ourselves ready. We have reason for joy and delight, now."
Hale Dwoskin, from The Sedona Method

"You are the ultimate joy. Looking for joy would be me looking for Lester. I am Lester. I don't have to go out there and look for him. If I am joy, I don't have to look for it out there. There's no need to go out for joy when it's inside you."
Lester Levenson, from Happiness Is Free, *volumes 1–5*

"When you find yourself wanting love, know that it is like a lake looking for water."
Hale Dwoskin

"The discovery that peace, happiness and love are ever-present within our own being and completely available at every moment of

experience, under all conditions, is the most important discovery that anyone can make."
Rupert Spira, from The Art of Peace and Happiness

Because happiness is your true nature, you can't acquire happiness; you can only BE it. If you are happy, you are being your true self, Awareness! When you are being the Awareness that you are you are in harmony with all of life, and to say your life will become magical is a colossal understatement.

"For that is when a human being comes fully alive: not at conception, not at birth, or maturity, nor at any of the ritualized moments we like to point to, the baptisms and weddings, bar mitzvahs and graduations. It comes when the sense of self crumbles, when wind is allowed to take the insubstantial thing we have believed ourselves to be. It is then that we truly live. It feels a bit like death (the person you have long been, after all, no longer exists), and yet . . . and yet . . . you find to your amazement that you have continued, that there is continuing life. There is life after death. You are finding out what is meant by heaven on earth."
Jan Frazier, from Opening the Door

Allow yourself to be happy. Allow yourself to be the happiness that you really are. Happiness is here right now. The power of Awareness is the answer to anything that threatens your happiness. If you open your attention and rest as the Awareness that you are, you will be happy!

If you're not feeling happy, remember to welcome any feeling that isn't happiness, and allow it to be present without trying to change it or get rid of it. As you welcome whatever feeling is present, you will feel it dissolve into the happiness that you really are.

Every time you open your arms and welcome an unhappy feeling, you are that much closer to lasting and permanent happiness, and that much closer to a harmonious, magical life. The more you welcome unhappy feelings, the more you will feel the happiness of your true self increasing every day. Eventually you will discover for yourself that underneath *every* unhappy feeling lies the never-ending happiness and love of Awareness.

CHAPTER 10 *Summary*

- *You* **are** *happiness. It is your true nature! Happiness—a never-ending wellspring of happiness—is here right now inside you!*

- *There's no other happiness but the happiness of your true self, Awareness. The happiness you have felt at any time in your life* **is** *the happiness of Awareness.*

- *There's nothing better for your life circumstances than you feeling happy. The happier you are, the more effortless is your life.*

- *When we seek happiness in the world, our happiness is fleeting.*

- *We can enjoy all the wonderful things that we want to be, do, or have in the world, but we can enjoy those things with the full knowledge that the only place to find real, permanent happiness is within us.*

- *Your thoughts determine how you're feeling, so if you're not happy it's because you're thinking about something you don't want.*

- *Standing between you and permanent happiness and who you really are is one thought—"I don't want this."*

- *When you feel pain or some hurt from a situation, let that hurtful feeling be a wake-up call telling you that right now you are believing negative thoughts that are not true.*

- *Many of us unintentionally resist being happy.*

- *Simply by realizing that we've been resisting happiness we take most of the power out of the suppressed belief that has been causing us to resist happiness.*

- *We don't have to do anything to be happy. Instead, we need to stop doing what we're doing that's making us unhappy.*

- *There is only one thing that causes unhappiness—attachment.*

- *Attachment comes when we hold on to something for fear of losing it because we believe that we can't be happy without it.*

- *Often our attachments make up the identity of the person we think we are, and we feel that if we dropped our attachments, we would lose our identity. So, we cling to our attachments, when all along they rob us of our happiness.*

- *What is actually attached is not* you, *but your mind. It's the mind that has attachments. Who you really are is not attached to a single thing.*

- *To free yourself of attachments all you have to do is just stay as Awareness, more and more, and all of your attachments will drop one by one.*

- *You can be happy in this very moment, no matter what is going on around you. Happiness is not something you have to look for or wait for.*

- *You can't acquire happiness; you can only BE it. If you are happy, you are being your true self.*

- *If you're not feeling happy, remember to welcome any feeling that isn't happiness, and allow it to be present without trying to change it or get rid of it.*

- *The more you welcome unhappy feelings, the more you will feel the happiness of your true self increasing every day.*

THE WORLD:
ALL IS WELL

"All shall be well, and all shall be well, and all manner of thing shall be well."
Juliana of Norwich

"You know, all mystics—Catholic, Christian, non-Christian, no matter what their theology, no matter what their religion—are unanimous on one thing; that all is well, all is well. Though everything is a mess, all is well. Strange paradox, to be sure. But, tragically, most people never get to see that all is well because they are asleep. They are having a nightmare."
Anthony de Mello, S.J., from Awareness: Conversations with the Masters

You might be thinking, how can everything be well when we look out into the world and see violence, wars, poverty, and destruction? People are fighting each other, attacking each other, arguing with each other, criticizing each other, and threatening each other, causing suffering across the planet.

But despite our turbulent history, when sages were asked how everything can possibly be well, they would answer with: "Because the world is an illusion."

What they mean by that is that the world is not what it appears to be. The world as we believe it to be—solid and concrete, out there existing separately from us, the only reality—is an illusion.

"There is no doubt whatsoever that the universe is the merest illusion."
Ramana Maharshi, from The Collected Works of Ramana Maharshi

We know from science that anything physical is mostly space; that the colors we see are actually the absence of those very colors; and the sounds we hear are really a vibration that our brain interprets into sounds through nerve signals. And we know that of all the mass of the Universe, only *0.005 percent* makes up the electromagnetic spectrum, and what's more, human beings can only perceive a *fraction* of that percentage. So, is the world really what it appears to be?

"Well, I look at the Empire State Building, you look at it, it looks probably the same to you and me, but what does it look like to an insect with 100 eyes? What does it look like to a snake that can only sense infrared? What does it look like to a bat that only knows the echo of ultrasound? So, the Empire State Building—the look of it—is a human look, it's not a crocodile look, and you can't assume the human sensory apparatus with its narrow bandwidth of experience is the only reality. Furthermore, you can't explain why the Empire State Building looks like what it is looking like if only photons are coming to your eyes."
Deepak Chopra™, M.D., from mindbodygreen *podcast*

When we investigate what we have assumed to be reality, we discover that our assumptions are not the facts we thought they were.

"Science starts with the assumption that the physical world is real, and that matter is real. Now, why that's a problem is, if you're a scientist, what is matter made of? They'll say, well, it's made of molecules. What are molecules made of? Atoms. What are atoms made of? Particles. What are particles made of? Then we get into situations of smaller particles. What are they made of? Well, if they're not being measured as particles they're waves of probability in mathematical space."
Deepak Chopra™, *M.D., from* mindbodygreen podcast

These waves of probability are not a material thing at all. They're just emptiness, and they only show up as particles when they're measured and observed by the mind!

"When you turn from one room to the next—when your animal senses no longer perceive the sounds of the dishwasher, the ticking clock, the smell of a chicken roasting—the kitchen and all its seemingly discrete bits dissolve into nothingness, or into waves of probability."
Robert Lanza, M.D.

With a lineage dating back to the fourteenth century, the Rose Cross Order describes the material world as nothing but "mental phantoms," and most certainly quantum physics confirms what the ancient traditions knew to be the truth.

When I first looked into quantum physics years ago, the research I read said that the room I am sitting in doesn't exist when I walk out of it because the room and everything in it falls back into a wave of probability when not observed. The room only reforms into particles of something solid when I walk back into it and I observe it. I used to have fun turning to walk out of the room and spinning around quickly to try and catch the room coming back into form. Not a chance!

"Before matter can peep forth—as a pebble, a snowflake, or even a subatomic particle—it has to be observed by a living creature."
Robert Lanza, M.D., from Biocentrism: How Life and Consciousness Are the Keys to Understanding the True Nature of the Universe

At its deepest level, the entire physical structure of our world and everything in it is nothing more than empty space. So, as Deepak says, "Is the world physical?"

But if the world isn't physical, then what is it?

All physical manifestation comes from mind. But it's much deeper than the idea of mind over matter; matter *is* mind. Everything appearing as solid and material—our whole physical world and Universe—is actually images projected by the mind.

"All is Mind; The Universe is mental . . . He who grasps the truth of the Mental Nature of the Universe is well advanced on The Path to Mastery."
From The Kybalion

"The world and the Universe are a mental concoction."
Lester Levenson, from Happiness Is Free, *volumes 1–5*

"Even the structure of the atom has been found by the mind."
Ramana Maharshi

"All manifestation is mind."
Francis Lucille

"Thought is the primary energy and vibration that emanated from God and is thus the creator of life, electrons, atoms, and all forms of energy."

Paramahansa Yogananda, from God Talks with Arjuna: The Bhagavad Gita

When you gaze out at the vast Universe at night, how certain are you that it's outside of you? We now know that any image we see comes from photons of light hitting our retinas, which then gets translated by the brain into an image. Our brain then flips the image and projects it from inside the back of our head. So even on a biological level we know that what we are seeing is actually within us.

When we look at the world, we're not seeing it from outside of us; we're seeing it from inside us. Our senses that detect the outside world are all experienced *inside* of us. When you touch something, you feel it from the inside of you, not the outside. Check for yourself. When someone puts their arms around you, you're seeing them and feeling the sensation of them from inside you. When you hear sounds, you're not hearing them from outside, but inside you. When you move your body, you feel and experience every sensation of movement from inside you. None of our senses or sensations prove that there's a world existing out there and separate from us.

"We concocted this whole universe and we've forgotten that we've done it. We say it is real and it is separate from me and all it really is is a picture in our mind. The only place where you'll see this world is in your mind. Put your mind to sleep and there's no more world. Don't wake up from sleep and there's no more world ever again— but you are."
Lester Levenson, from Will Power *audio*

All that you see, from a teaspoon to the sun in the sky, is a projection of the mind. Just like a movie projector, our mind projects the pictures of our world. It's like standing in a 360-degree theater with images above, below, and all around you, with full surround sound. It makes for a very convincing experience.

"The world existing as an independent reality is an illusion."
Francis Lucille

The world as you see it—a world that appears to exist outside our bodies and independently of us—is an illusion created by the mind. The appearance of things being solid is an illusion created by the mind. The appearance of things being three-dimensional is an illusion created by the mind.

The images of the world and our experience of it through our senses is just like the dream world when you're asleep. The contents of your dream and your experience of the dream are entirely mind-made, just as your experience of the world when you're awake takes place entirely in your mind.

"Knowing that our mind possesses this wonderful power of creation and self-deception, is it not reasonable for us to suspect that the body we take to be 'I' and the world we take to be real in our present waking state may in fact be nothing more than a mere imagination or mental projection, just like the body and world that we experience in dream? What evidence do we have that the body and world we experience in this waking state are anything other than a creation of our own mind?"
Michael James, from Happiness and the Art of Being

"In your imagination you have written and projected a cinema show of actors, acts, and audiences on a screen and have lost sight of the fact that it is all in your mind."
Lester Levenson, from Happiness Is Free, *volumes 1–5*

"The world is made of thoughts and ideas."
My teacher

"What we're seeing out there is our own mind."
Lester Levenson, from Happiness Is Free, *volumes 1–5*

"Everything that we've given a name to—latitude, longitude, Greenwich meantime, nations, states, stars, galaxies, everything you've given a name to—is a human construct. So, we created this world . . . over thousands of years. We are the storytellers."
Deepak Chopra™, *M.D., from SAND Conference talk, 2018*

We not only created this world through our individual thought and collective thought, but we're creating everything we're experiencing from moment to moment.

"The appearance called the world? The world is only an illusion that we created. Some day you will discover that you created this entire universe . . . which is nothing but a composite of all of our thoughts."

Lester Levenson, from Will Power *audio*

And what is the power that can turn thoughts into an apparent world and Universe? It's Infinite Awareness, the only power there is. Infinite Awareness is the one and only power in existence; it has no competition. And you are that.

It's All Consciousness-Awareness

"The world is not, on the whole, the place described in our schoolbooks. For several centuries, starting roughly with the Renaissance, a single mindset about the construct of the cosmos has dominated scientific thought. This model has brought us untold insights into the nature of the universe—and countless applications that have transformed every aspect of our lives. But this model is reaching the end of its useful life and needs to be replaced with a radically different paradigm that reflects a deeper reality, one totally ignored until now."

Robert Lanza, M.D., from Biocentrism: How Life and Consciousness Are the Keys to Understanding the True Nature of the Universe

"For some inexplicable reason the most common element in every possible experience—consciousness—has kept itself a secret."
Deepak Chopra™, M.D.

In his talks, Deepak Chopra raises the two biggest hard problems of science that remain unsolved:

1. What is the substance of the Universe?

2. Where does consciousness come from?

"Science cannot solve the ultimate mystery of nature. And that is because, in the last analysis, we ourselves are part of nature and therefore part of the mystery that we are trying to solve."
Max Planck, quantum physicist, from Where Is Science Going?

While scientists continue to believe in a model of the world that is objective, material, solid, and existing separately from us, they won't find the truth of what the underlying substance of the Universe is. But for hundreds of years sages have known the answer to the biggest unanswered questions of science.

What is the substance of the Universe?
Consciousness is the substance of the Universe.

Where does consciousness come from?
Consciousness doesn't come from anywhere—everything comes from Consciousness.

Consciousness or Awareness is infinite—it is everywhere at the same time—so how could it come from anywhere?

We know from science that our material Universe had a beginning with the Big Bang, which means it must have an end, something that scientists anticipate. With a beginning and an end, that makes our Universe finite, and so if it is finite it must have come from something that is *infinite*! The Universe came out of Consciousness, and Consciousness, which is infinite, is the very foundation and underlying substance of our Universe and everything in it.

You are Infinite Consciousness, Infinite Awareness, which means that ultimately, the Universe *is you*, *in you*.

"The whole universe is contained within a single human being—you."
Rumi

The world, the Universe, and everything in it, including your body, are *in* Awareness. They are all sitting in and on Awareness. Awareness is omnipresent; it is everywhere, and everything is in it and arises out of it. Awareness is omniscient; it knows everything, because it contains everything. Awareness is omnipotent; it is all power, because there is no other power than it.

"You, yourself are the eternal energy, which appears as this universe."
Alan Watts, from Nature of Consciousness

The World Movie

When we go to see a movie, or watch television, we wouldn't be able to see the pictures if the screen wasn't there. The mind also needs a screen to be able to see the pictures of the world movie that it's projecting. And that screen is Awareness.

The world movie that our mind projects is sitting in and on the screen of Awareness, which means that what we call the world is ultimately made of Awareness—the one and only Infinite Awareness that we are. When the sages say, "We are one" and "We are everything," this is what they're referring to. We *are* absolutely everything, because we are the one Awareness within which and upon which everything exists!

"So, all this manifestation is really nothing. It is really only that space-like-awareness vibrating into patterns, shapes and forms."
Sailor Bob Adamson, from What's Wrong with Right Now?

"The underlying state of consciousness is like the atmosphere in which all these other things take place, the movie screen on which they play. Nothing affects it. Nothing touches it."
Jan Frazier, from When Fear Falls Away

"Nothing is as it appears to be, and You are not as you appear to be. You only have to look a little deeper and feel a little deeper."
Pamela Wilson

Wanting to Change the World?

"Change in society is of secondary importance; that will come about naturally, inevitably, when you as a human being bring about the change in yourself."
J. Krishnamurti, from the third public talk, Santa Monica, 1970

"Awareness is what we are. You didn't come to save the world—you came to love the world."
Anthony de Mello, S.J.

"You want the world to be different. Let us assume that you were given the power to erase the world as it is and reconstruct it as you would like it to be: no wars, no tyrants, no mosquitoes, no cancer, no pain, and everybody smiles. You would end up with something that is very boring, something with no flavor. Then you start adding a bit of salt and pepper, and at the end, you would be back where you started, having realized that it was perfect the way it was!"
Francis Lucille, from The Perfume of Silence

While we remain attached to our own beliefs and the belief that we are separate individuals, the world will never be at peace. Billions of egos will always create strife because egos are unstable—they will never agree. But Awareness allows for all of it. Awareness allows for the illusion, the false beliefs, the lack of peace, the strife, the suffering, and the wars, because only love allows everything to exist. Your freedom from any suffering doesn't depend on the world coming to peace, but depends on your seeing that you have mistaken yourself for only a person, and on your experiencing yourself as the one and only Infinite Being.

"The infinite Being isn't concerned about calamity in the world as it's never affected by any of those things."
David Bingham

"When you see the world as you, it will look entirely different from what it looked like when it appeared separate. You will love and identify with it and everyone in it."
Lester Levenson, from Happiness Is Free, *volumes 1–5*

"As we become more conscious, more love arises. With self-realization, there is a realization that everything is you, so it isn't possible to harm anything."
David Bingham

Awareness says "Yes" to absolutely everything. Awareness allows for the freedom of everything to be the way it is, because the world and everything in it *is* Awareness—its own self, our own self. That means there can be nothing to oppose us. No calamity can befall us. No atomic bombs or meteors can destroy us. No lack or limitation can possibly affect us. Because when you boil it right down, all of it is *us*. And when you have realized your true self, and you are resting as that Awareness, you will know:

No matter how things appear in the world, all is always, always well.

CHAPTER 11 *Summary*

- *The world as we believe it to be—solid and concrete, out there existing separately from us, the only reality—is an illusion.*

- *At its deepest level, the entire physical structure of our world and everything in it is nothing more than empty space.*

- *Matter is mind. Everything appearing as solid and material—our whole physical world and Universe—is actually images projected by the mind.*

- *The contents of your dream and your experience of the dream are entirely mind-made, just as your experience of the world when you're awake takes place entirely in your mind.*

- *The power that can turn thoughts into an apparent Universe is Infinite Awareness, the only power there is.*

- *The Universe came out of Consciousness, and Consciousness, which is infinite, is the very foundation and underlying substance of our Universe and everything in it.*

- *The world, the Universe, and everything in it, including your body, are in Awareness. They are all sitting in and on Awareness.*

- *While we remain attached to our own beliefs and the belief that we are separate individuals, the world will never be at peace. Billions of egos will always create strife.*

- *Your freedom from any suffering doesn't depend on the world coming to peace; it depends on your seeing that you have mistaken yourself for only a person, and on your experiencing yourself as the one and only Infinite Being.*

- *Awareness says "Yes" to absolutely everything. Awareness allows for the freedom of everything to be the way it is, because the world, and everything in it, is Awareness—its own self.*

- *No matter how things appear in the world, all is always, always well.*

CHAPTER 12

THE END—
THERE IS
NO END

What if the one thing that we're all so afraid of isn't true? What if there is no such thing as death as we think of it? What if when we die we wake up?

"Whence come I and whither go I? That is the great unfathomable question, the same for every one of us. Science has no answer to it."
Max Planck, quantum physicist

"The body dies, but the spirit that transcends it cannot be touched by death."
Ramana Maharshi, from The Collected Works of Ramana Maharshi

"If you take yourself to be the body and mind only, that 'you' will certainly die! When you discover yourself as unborn and imperishable awareness, the fear of death will trouble you no longer. In fact, this is the death of death."
Mooji

"When you wake up, all fear, including the fear of physical death, goes away. This is because what 'you' have turned out to be isn't something that's subject to harm."
Jan Frazier, from The Freedom of Being

"Death is a stripping away of all that is not you. The secret of life is to 'die before you die'—and find that there is no death."
Eckhart Tolle, from The Power of Now

To die before you die means to bring an end to the mind's delusion that you are just a person. It means to die to the *idea* of being a person, and to realize the Infinite Awareness that you really are. Only then will you "die before you die" and discover the truth—that there is no death.

"Of all the things human beings can learn in this life, I have the greatest news to tell you, the most beautiful thing to share: You are that which is formless, unchanging, and never dies."
Mooji, from White Fire, *second edition*

"You, your body mind, and the world that you see are all part of the same virtual reality . . . You—the real you—is formless consciousness, and once you identify with that, you see every other identity you had is provisional. Whether it's husband or father, or son, or wife . . . all these are provisional identities that have a birth and a death, and they keep transforming, they're not real. . . . The only absolute identity you have is infinite, formless, inconceivable being that morphs itself into any reality based on its constructs."
Deepak Chopra™, M.D., from mindbodygreen *podcast*

"We have forgotten that we are this consciousness and have identified ourselves with objects. We think, 'I am the body, therefore I am going to die.' However, consciousness doesn't find itself in a body. The body appears in consciousness, the mind appears in consciousness, the world appears in consciousness. That is our experience. In spite of this, we superimpose the opposite notion onto

our experience, that consciousness is in the mind, that the mind is in the body, and that the body is in the world."
Francis Lucille, from The Perfume of Silence

"You are now thinking that you are the body and therefore confuse yourself with its birth and death. But you are not the body and you have no birth and death."
Ramana Maharshi, from Be as You Are

"So the real answer to death is, it's another human construct. If you believe in the physical world then you have to believe in death, and you have to believe in birth, but understand that you are a formless being—*formless*—that experiences itself as form. So right now that formless being is experiencing itself as a body mind."
Deepak Chopra™, M.D., from mindbodygreen *podcast*

"You have agreed that you will die only because you have accepted from someone that you were born."
Sri Poonja (Papaji), from The Truth Is

"There was never a time when I did not exist, nor you . . . nor is there any future in which we shall cease to be."
Krishna

It's impossible to imagine not being, because you can never *not* be. If you imagine not being, there's an Awareness that you're imagining not being, and there you are—Awareness!

"So, when you are a baby you don't know this is a table or this is a hand or that you have a body. All your experience is . . . a gooey universe with lots of colors, sensations, images, no thoughts yet,

just a sense of wonder and confusion. Then we introduce concepts; you're a male, you're American, you're human, that's a star, that's a galaxy, that's the planet earth. That is how the scientific worldview works. So, you are suddenly now looking at the world through a filter. Consciousness has become a conditioned mind that is giving you an experience of a physical world and a physical body, and now because you've constructed this thing in your consciousness, now you're worried about birth, death. These are human concepts. There is no birth, there is no death, there is no physical body, there is no Universe. There is consciousness and it's infinite and you're IT."
Deepak Chopra™, *M.D., from* mindbodygreen *podcast*

"Immortality is attained in proportion as personal sense is overcome . . . As we put off the personal ego and attain the consciousness of our real Self . . . we attain immortality. And that can be achieved here and now."
Joel S. Goldsmith, from The Infinite Way

"Death is not extinguishing the light; it is only putting out the lamp because the dawn has come."
Rabindranath Tagore

What is it like for somebody who dies?

"It's the same as waking up after a dream. No different at all."
My teacher

The teachers tell us emphatically that Awareness or Consciousness was never born and never dies. That means that when the body ends, Awareness and Consciousness remain as always—fully aware and fully alive. It's then that you may realize you were never the body, because you find yourself to be fully aware and existing like before, except without a body. Awareness doesn't need a body to be aware. When the body ends, there is not a single second that you are not aware—not a trillionth of a second that you don't remain fully aware. You are eternally and infinitely aware, fully and completely alive, with a body or without a body.

"Consciousness and awareness never began, and will never end."
Robert Lanza, M.D., from Biocentrism: How Life and Consciousness Are the Keys to Understanding the True Nature of the Universe

"Life has no opposite. The opposite of death is birth. Life is eternal."
Eckhart Tolle, from Stillness Speaks

How would your life be different if you actually knew that no one dies? What if you knew with certainty that you and everyone else are the one eternal Infinite Being? What would life be like for you if you lived with that knowledge, knowing it is the truth?

The sages tell us that when we know the truth, life becomes light and full of ease. There is a lot of laughter, unbridled love, and total enjoyment of everything that happens. Every moment is savored, and there's an overwhelming appreciation for the wonder and splendor of the manifestation of the world. A deep love and compassion for humanity and every living thing arises.

The sages tell us that we will be unruffled by people or things that used to bother us. We won't see problems anymore or find things to be serious the way we once thought they were. We will look lightly upon all the comings and goings of the world, as though it were a movie that we were watching. And we will be filled with unutterable peace knowing that despite everything that is happening, there is no end for us or anyone.

From the time I discovered The Secret I knew that we couldn't die. Once I understood that there are laws governing our thought and our physical life, like cause and effect, attraction, and karma, I knew we had to live beyond this lifetime; otherwise, what would be the point? How could anyone master the laws in one lifetime? Even the Buddha said he lived five hundred lifetimes before he realized who he really is, and that's the Buddha!

"The feeling 'I' as you use it to mean your individuality will never, ever leave you. It expands. What happens as you discover what you are is that you begin to see that others are you, that you are me, that there is only One, that you are now and always have been that one and glorious Infinite Being."
Lester Levenson, from Happiness Is Free, *volumes 1–5*

Avatar

"All of this is the game that consciousness is playing: the game of disguising itself, pretending that it is really a person."
David Bingham

"Our essential nature of pure Awareness gains or loses nothing from the entire human adventure."
Rupert Spira, from The Ashes of Love

Having a life on earth is like having an avatar in a computer game. When your body dies in a computer game, you get a new body and you go back into the game, with one avatar after another, until you finish the game. Some traditions tell us that in our human life we also get a new body every time we die, until we "finish the game" by waking up and fully realizing who we are—Awareness.

We've most likely all lived many lifetimes, most likely hundreds and hundreds of them. But it's waking up to the truth that Consciousness and the Universe delight in; and that makes *this* lifetime the most important one!

"You are here to enable the divine purpose of the universe to unfold. That is how important you are!"
Eckhart Tolle, from The Power of Now

You have to realize the truth for yourself because this can't be given to you. How can anyone give you, to you? You are already You! Someone can only point you in the direction of where to look. It's from your *own experience* that you must realize this, not from anyone's words.

"You and the world and the entire universe are modifications of awareness. You and the universe are awareness in motion."
Deepak Chopra™, M.D., from mindbodygreen *podcast*

"What you are basically deep, deep down, far, far in, is simply the fabric and structure of existence itself."
Alan Watts, from Out of Your Mind

"When we truly feel that the universe is in us, is us, that there is no separation, that there is this wholeness, then the universe and the events in the world unfold in accordance with this perspective, which is the true perspective. They reveal the sanctity, the holiness of the world. They reveal the permanent miracle. First it is experienced as a feeling and later on, it is confirmed by our experience of the world."

Francis Lucille, from The Perfume of Silence

Human Being to Infinite Being

My teacher says that to realize the Infinite Being that we are is just a decision. There's only one decision maker and it's you, the Infinite Being—so therefore the decision to fully realize who you are is no different from the decision to get a glass of water. You can make the decision: "I intend to be fully conscious of my true nature, Awareness. I intend to fulfill my purpose and live my life in the joy of the Infinite Awareness that I am. I have made the decision to fully realize the eternal, indestructible pure Awareness that I am."

"Take all your wanting, all your restless maneuvering, the entire terrible weight and noise of it. Put it in a box and tape it shut. Load the box onto a truck driving away from you and never coming back. There is something left, isn't there? You are still here. You can feel yourself being. Welcome home."

Jan Frazier, from The Freedom of Being

Our incredible journey together through this book has been to point you in the direction that will take you from believing you are only a human being to realizing the Infinite Being that you truly are; to show you the way from suffering to a life of blissful happiness and peace; and to free you from hurt, upset, anxiety, worry, and problems, so that you instead exist in the continuous happiness of Awareness. Your true self, Awareness, is the *only* permanence in existence. Everything else comes and goes, appears and disappears, but you are the one that never came and never goes. Awareness is the one that is aware of every second of your life experience, yet isn't affected or harmed by it, and welcomes everything in it.

"We are living through the most exciting, challenging and most critical time in human history. Never before has so much been possible; and never before has so much been at stake."
Peter Russell, author and retired physicist

Through the words of the aware beings shared in this book, you have begun to wake up, and no matter where you go from here that can never be lost. Where before the mind's elaborate illusion might have been seamless, now there is a tear in its fabric. That tear can never seal completely, leaving your mind in the darkness of ignorance again. Awareness, the Infinite Being that you are, will ensure that the fabric of illusion will continue to tear until the truth is fully revealed and realized, and you are finally reunited as your true self.

"When we take one step toward the Self, It takes nine steps towards us."
Lester Levenson, from Happiness Is Free, *volumes 1–5*

Some people may wake up on the spot while reading this book, but for most of us, it seems to be a journey of awakening. While you continue to let go of negative feelings and beliefs and continue to practice staying as Awareness the best you can, Awareness will keep expanding within you. Eventually Awareness will expand so much within you that you will recognize that the whole Universe and everything in it is contained in you.

It's a journey to nowhere, as there's nowhere for you to go; you are already everything that you're looking for, right here, right now. As Rupert Spira says, "There's nowhere to go. Just try and take a step toward yourself. You can't do it."

The Infinite Being that you are is present right now. If you don't re-alize it fully yet, it's simply that your mind has convinced you that you're a person. But that is changing right now.

"When the Self has been realized, we can never go back to not knowing what it is. We can, however, choose to become absorbed in individuality again."
David Bingham

Watch the mind, because it will try and tell you all kinds of things, like, "You don't want this—it would be boring being Awareness all the time! Let's go out and meet up with Tom for some fun!" Of course, fun is good too, and who you really are delights in fun. When you are living as your true self, Awareness, you'll still have fun and meet up with Tom. In fact, as Awareness, you will have even more fun than you've ever had. You will laugh a lot. You will do all the things you did before. The only difference is that you will do everything in con-tinuous happiness and peace, with no fear, worry, stress, or sadness.

"Even if you became an astronaut and discovered unknown galaxies, it would not be as great as discovering your own Self right here on earth."
Mooji, from White Fire, *second edition*

I want you to understand that the Infinite Being that you are is the "you" that you feel yourself to be *right now*. There isn't another ver-sion of you that you have to become first, in order to be the Infinite

Being. When I first made this discovery, I was looking for another version of me for quite a long time, until I realized that it's the Infinite Being who is the one who is aware through my body right now.

"You are Divine. It's time to start being that; quit pretending you're not."
Pamela Wilson

Who Are You?

"We are all Gods acting like goddamned fools."
Lester Levenson

"The only purpose in life—the sole purpose—is to be the totality of who we are. It is our secret intention, and we will knock off any props we think are necessary to achieve our purpose—marriages, houses, loved ones, even if that prop is the body itself."
My teacher

When marriages end, or we lose loved ones, or things seem to fall apart in our lives, we may suffer a lot, but very often it's through our suffering that we begin to wonder what life is all about. Many of the enlightened sages have gone through immense suffering, and it was their suffering that led them to question life intensely, and which ulti-mately led them to the truth of who they are.

It can be difficult in the midst of suffering to even consider that the suffering you are going through is leading you to something won-drous, but indeed for many their suffering has led them right into the paradise of their very own self.

"How suffering becomes a door to peace. How pain is a trapdoor that if stood fully upon opens under the terrible weight of full acceptance . . . How the very things we think are obstacles to peace are windows, and on the other side of the windows are our peaceful selves. How if we do not get this, the obstacles will keep coming and keep coming. How we pull them to us like iron filings to a magnet. How powerful is a human being. How little we know this. How the not-knowing is the greatest obstacle of all."
Jan Frazier, from When Fear Falls Away

But now you know.

"You are eternally yourself. The rest is only a dream. This is why true self-discovery is called awakening."
Mooji

"It's only a dream" is the truth behind everything you see and experience. This discovery does not mean that when a person is struggling due to difficult circumstances that you will lack compassion. However, when you know the truth, the serenity and peace emanating from you will surround them, comfort them, and penetrate them without any need for words. When you know that all is well no matter what, you are finally free from any notion of negativity, and your presence will soothe others tremendously in their suffering. It is claimed that one individual who is living fully as Infinite Awareness counteracts the negativity of millions and millions of people. Such is the power of the pure love of Awareness.

"You are God in a physical body. You are Spirit in the flesh. You are Eternal Life expressing itself as You. You are a cosmic being. You

are all power. You are all wisdom. You are all intelligence. You are perfection. You are magnificence."
From The Secret

You are the space-like Awareness that's holding planet earth, the sun, stars, galaxies, and the Universe in place. You are the substratum of existence.

"You keep trying to go left or right or outward but the answer to everything is who you really are. And everything in the world is pointing you back to yourself."
My teacher

"Nothing and no one can complete you. You are already whole and complete exactly as you are right here and now."
Hale Dwoskin

"By God, when you see your beauty you will be the idol of yourself."
Rumi

"All you have to do is discover what you've already got. That is why it is called 'realization': you realize what is already there, what has been there right along."
Jan Frazier, from When Fear Falls Away

For as long as human beings have inhabited planet earth, they've been asking the same three questions. Who am I? Where did I come from? Where do I go to? The answer to all three is: Awareness, Awareness, Awareness.

"From bliss all beings are born; in bliss they live; to bliss they return."
Taittiriya Upanishad

Welcome home, to the place you never left.

"Don't worry about anything at all. You are not here by accident. This form is just a costume for a while. But the one who is behind the costume, this one is eternal. You must know this. If you know this and trust this, you don't have to worry about anything."
Mooji, from White Fire, *second edition*

"What happened to me can happen to you. You may not believe it is possible to become free, to cease suffering, to have joy running like a warm stream beneath every day, no matter what the day brings you. But I'm here to tell you it is possible."
Jan Frazier, from When Fear Falls Away

With your mind stilled, the Infinite Being that you are, who knows everything, is in charge.

"When you are permanently being who you are—consciousness-awareness—you will receive the answer to every single question you have. Every desire you've ever had will be fulfilled."
My teacher

You will have complete clarity. You will never again suffer from confusion or uncertainty.

"We're supposed to function completely from intuition. The moment you act from the intuition that you are, your life will be beautiful."
My teacher

All suffering can end for you right here, right now. Awareness is your way out of all suffering; it is your key to immortality, and a life of laughter, joy, sheer abundance, beauty, and bliss.

"The light of one human being who discovers the truth has been lighting human existence for thousands of years. Such is the power of a human being who realizes the truth of who they are."
Mooji

"There were people who were not widely known in their lifetimes who nonetheless exerted a great influence for good. There were many more whose names are not found in the historical record. Although they have been forgotten, the intelligence and love that they released into the world is still reaching us. Our true gift to the world is to be a source of love and clarity, and to recognize that to be this source one has to know oneself intimately."
Francis Lucille, from Truth Love Beauty

"One individual with nothing but love can stand up against the entire world because this love is so powerful. This love is nothing but the Self. This love is God."
Lester Levenson, from Happiness Is Free, *volumes 1–5*

There's only one source of perfection, and that source is you! When you see love anywhere in the world, realize it is you. When you behold a beautiful sunset, know the beauty you behold is you. When you notice happiness anywhere in the world, recognize it is you. Where there is laughter, know that it is the endless joy of you shining through. When you look out at the spectacular myriad of life-forms in the world, know that the life that is breathing them is the Infinite Being, and that is also you. There's nothing else in existence but the glory of the one and only Infinite Being, the true self, pure Awareness-Consciousness. And it is you.

Ultimately, every moment and every circumstance of your life is pointing you to home—to Awareness. When anything hurts you in life, without exception it's a wake-up call telling you you're going in the wrong direction—you're believing something that isn't true. We are the prodigal son. At times we've staggered, we've been bruised and beaten, we've been scared, we've suffered, and we've fallen down many times, but the end for all of us is to realize, to remember, and to recognize who we truly are—eternal Awareness—and that there is no end for any of us.

This is the simple but wondrous truth that has been known by so few. This is The Greatest Secret.

No End

∞

CHAPTER 12 *Summary*

- *There is no such thing as death as we think of it. The body dies, but the spirit cannot be touched by death.*

- *To die before you die means to die to the* idea *of being a person, and to realize the Infinite Awareness that you really are.*

- *When the body ends, Awareness and Consciousness remain as always— fully aware and fully alive.*

- *When we know the truth, life becomes light and full of ease. There is a lot of laughter, unbridled love, and total enjoyment of everything that happens. A deep love and compassion arise for humanity and every living thing.*

- *Your real self is the* only *permanence in existence. Everything else comes and goes, appears and disappears.*

- *Having a life on earth is like having an avatar in a computer game. In our human life we also get a new body every time we die, until we "finish the game" by waking up and fully realizing who we are—Awareness.*

- *As your true self you will have even more fun than you've ever had. You will do all the things you did before. The only difference is that you will do everything in continuous happiness and peace.*

- *The only purpose in life is to be the totality of who we are.*

- *Very often it's through our suffering that we begin to wonder what life is all about. For many, their suffering has led them right into the paradise of their very own self.*

- *When you know that all is well no matter what, you are finally free from any notion of negativity, and your presence will soothe others tremendously in their suffering.*

- *Awareness is your way out of all suffering; it is your key to immortality, and a life of laughter, joy, abundance, beauty, and bliss.*

- *When you see love anywhere in the world, realize it is* you.

- *When anything hurts you in life, without exception it's a wake-up call telling you you're going in the wrong direction—you're believing something that isn't true.*

- *The end for all of us is to realize, to remember, and to recognize who we truly are—eternal Awareness.*

THE GREATEST SECRET

Practices

Affirmation:
"I intend to be fully conscious of my true nature, Awareness.
I intend to fulfill my purpose and live my life in the joy of the
Infinite Awareness that I am. I have made the decision to be the
eternal, indestructible pure Awareness that I am."

- *The Awareness Practice*
  Step 1. Ask yourself, "Am I aware?"
  Step 2. Notice Awareness.
  Step 3. Stay as Awareness.

- *Shift your attention to Awareness by noticing Awareness multiple times throughout the day.*

- *Give five minutes a day, at the very least, to putting your attention on Awareness. You can do it when you first wake up, when you get into bed, or at any other time that suits you.*

- *Question every negative feeling with: "Am I that, or am I the one that is aware of it?"*

- *You can use the same question ("Am I that, or am I the one that is aware of it?") for any negative thoughts or painful body sensations.*

- *The Super Practice*
  Step 1. Welcome anything negative.
  Step 2. Stay as Awareness.

- *Ask yourself this question: "Am I the one suffering, or am I the one that is aware of the suffering?" The truth is that you are the one that is* aware of *the suffering, rather than the one suffering.*

- *Be very aware when you hear yourself say, "I believe" or "I don't believe," because immediately following those words is a belief.*

- *Be very aware when you hear yourself say, "I think" or "I don't think," because most likely what will follow that will also reveal a belief.*

- *You can give the subconscious mind an instruction to highlight your beliefs for you, so you can become more aware of them: "Show me my beliefs clearly one by one, so I become aware of each and every one of them."*

- *To expose your beliefs, become aware of your reactions.*

- *Welcome any and all feelings of resistance.*

- *To free yourself of any attachments or problems, welcome them and just stay as Awareness.*

- *If you're not feeling happy, remember to welcome any feeling that isn't happiness, and allow it to be present without trying to change it or get rid of it.*

- *Awareness says "Yes" to absolutely everything. Awareness allows for the freedom of everything to be the way it is, because the world, and everything in it, is Awareness—its own self.*

- *Stop and be present right now, because Awareness can only be recognized in this present moment!*

*"Whatever comes your way,
this causeless joy will hold."*

—Jan Frazier

Featured in

THE GREATEST SECRET

I feel incredibly fortunate and grateful to be on the planet at the same time as the amazing living teachers featured in this book. Every one of these beings dedicates their life to *our* freedom and *our* happiness. And for many of them, they have been doing this for decades. If you were in the presence of any one of them, you would feel the overwhelming love and joy emanating from them, reflecting back your true nature to you. If you have the opportunity to be with one of the teachers in person, take it! And if you cannot be with them in person, you can most certainly connect with some of them live online. It's the next best thing.

Waking up to our true nature is easier now than it has ever been; it is possible for every one of us to go all the way home. It may not be as easy in the future—we don't know—so if you can, make the most of this time now, your life now, and these inspirational teachers.

SAILOR BOB ADAMSON

Sailor Bob is Australian and resides in my hometown of Melbourne. I only became aware of Sailor Bob in early 2016, after I had realized the truth of who we really are. I was living in the United States at that time, yet many years earlier when I was still living in Melbourne I had passed Sailor Bob's home day after day, year after year, when traveling to work. I had no idea I was driving past a self-realized teacher, someone who would one day play an integral role in my life. When I found out about Sailor Bob in 2016, I decided to get on a plane immediately and go and see him. He was in his eighties at that time, and I attended several of his meetings and had personal one-on-one meetings with him. Each time I saw Sailor Bob I felt lighter, happier, and freer. It was early days for me in my spiritual awakening, and I struggled to grasp everything he told me, yet today all of it is crystal clear. Sailor Bob realized his true nature many decades earlier while in India, as a disciple of Nisargadatta Maharaj. Since that time, Bob has shared his teachings from his home to anyone who is interested in hearing the truth. He is in his nineties now, and still continues to hold meetings in his home. His words, "What's wrong if you don't think about it?" are some of the simplest and most profound words ever given. Sailor Bob's books are *What's Wrong with Right Now?* and *Presence-Awareness: Just This and Nothing Else.* You can enjoy more of the precious Sailor Bob Adamson on his website: sailorbobadamson.com.

JULIAN BARBOUR

Julian Barbour is a British physicist. He is the author of three books: *The End of Time: The Next Revolution in Our Understanding of the Universe*, which explores the idea that time is an illusion; *The Discovery of Dynamics,* which investigates the background to Newton's discoveries; and his latest book, *The Janus Point,* which he completed at age eighty-three. Julian's website is: platonia.com.

DAVID BINGHAM

David Bingham is British. He spent decades as a spiritual seeker, and it was listening to a podcast of the teacher John Wheeler that woke him up to who he really is. David was interviewed on Conscious TV to share his experience of self-realization, and it was that very interview that began my awakening. I watched the interview, I followed David's footsteps and listened to the same podcast, and I then had a phone consultation with David in which he helped me experience Awareness, and see the truth of who I really am. David is now a teacher and he has been able to help many realize their true nature. David's interviews on Conscious TV are also available in the book *Conversations on Non-duality.* You can find out more about the wonderful David Bingham's teachings on his website: nonconceptualawareness.com.

DEEPAK CHOPRA™, M.D., FACP

Deepak Chopra™, a board-certified endocrinologist, made a journey of discovery from India to the United States, and after becoming disenchanted with Western medicine he moved to integrative whole-health medicine. In 1995 Deepak opened the Chopra Center for Wellbeing, which transformed to Chopra Global, a whole-health company that is empowering personal transformation for the wellbeing of millions of people globally. He has written more than ninety books, many of them bestsellers. I first saw Deepak speak at the Science and Nonduality (SAND) Conference several years ago, where I leapt to my feet in a standing ovation after he finished speaking. You can find Deepak's extensive and prolific teachings on his website: deepakchopra.com.

ANTHONY DE MELLO, S.J.

The late Anthony (Tony) de Mello was a Jesuit priest born in Bombay, India. Although he was only on the planet for forty-five years, his teachings are as much alive today as they ever were. Tony's unique ability of joining Western and Eastern spirituality made his teachings inspirational and transformative. Much of his audience was Catholic or Christian, and he drew a great deal from the teachings in the Bible, illuminating their meaning for his audiences. It was this in conjunction with his brilliant storytelling that woke people up to the truth. Tony's books have remained bestsellers since the death of his physical form in 1987, and have sold millions of copies: *The Way to Love, Sadhana, A Way to God, One Minute Wisdom, Heart of the Enlightened, Wellsprings, Song of the Bird,* and *Taking Flight.* My favorites to begin with are *Awareness: Conversations with the Masters* and *Rediscovering Life.* There are also video recordings available, and it is a joy to witness Tony's teachings, which always came with a smile in his voice and with love in his heart. This wonderful teacher's website is demellospirituality.com.

HALE DWOSKIN

Hale Dwoskin was a student and the designated heir of the legendary Lester Levenson, and he was also one of the featured teachers in *The Secret*. Hale has dedicated his life to continuing Lester's work through the Sedona Method, helping others realize their true nature. The success of the method is proven through the transformation of many people's lives. Hale holds regular retreats where he trains people how to release negativity so they can realize their true self. A big part of my own journey has been releasing. You can find all of Hale's and Lester's teachings in the books *The Sedona Method* and *Happiness Is Free*, volumes 1–5. Hale does several retreats a year in the United States, where he resides, and worldwide. His talks, teleconferences, and retreats are made available for people all around the world to join online, and I have attended many of them that way. All of this wonderful material is also archived and available on Hale's website: sedona.com.

PETER DZIUBAN

Peter Dziuban is an author and lecturer on Awareness, Consciousness, and spirituality. American born, Peter lives in Arizona. I first heard about Peter when my teacher recommended his book *Consciousness Is All*. I read the book and then listened to the audio of the book in which Peter spontaneously gives many more hours of teachings. *Consciousness Is All* is insightful and breathtaking—it will literally take your breath away multiple times throughout. I am truly grateful for having experienced this book because it shattered my world (a good thing!). If you are ready to take a more advanced step, it is a must read. In the meantime, if you are a beginner and would like to sample Peter's teachings in a simpler form, I would recommend you start with his book *Simply Notice*. His website is peterdziuban.com.

JAN FRAZIER

Jan Frazier, a writer, teacher, and mother, experienced a radical transformation of consciousness in 2003. She had spent years in extreme fear over a possible cancer diagnosis, when suddenly fear fell away from her, and she was immersed in a state of causeless joy that has never left her. As she continued her life, she discovered it is possible to live a richly human life free of suffering. Her wish now is to communicate the truth that is within every person. I have been fortunate enough to connect with Jan in a private session, and I have read every one of her beautiful books. *When Fear Falls Away: The Story of a Sudden Awakening* is her day-by-day account of her awakening. Her other books are *The Freedom of Being: At Ease with What Is*, *The Great Sweetening: Life After Thought*, and *Opening the Door: Jan Frazier Teachings on Awakening*. Jan is a very accessible, poetic, and exquisitely beautiful writer, as testified by the quotes in this book, which she so graciously allowed me to include. You can find out more about Jan's teachings on her website: janfrazierteachings.com.

JOEL GOLDSMITH

Joel Goldsmith was a much-loved American spiritual author and mystic. He is best known for his book *The Infinite Way*, which became a classic and has impacted the lives of many people around the world, including mine. Joel has many books, and original recordings of his talks are available on his website, lovingly preserved by his three children: joelgoldsmith.com.

DR. DAVID R. HAWKINS, M.D., PH.D.

Dr. Hawkins was a nationally renowned American psychiatrist, physician, researcher, spiritual teacher, and lecturer. Because of Dr. Hawkins's scientific and medical background, his spiritual teachings were scientifically compelling. I first heard of Dr. Hawkins over fifteen years ago when I read his book *Power vs Force*, which impacted me greatly. It was years later that I would once again follow his teachings when I listened to many of his lectures and read his book *Letting Go*. Other books by Dr. David Hawkins are *Book of Slides*; *Healing and Recovery*; *Reality, Spirituality and Modern Man*; *Transcending the Levels of Consciousness*; *Discovery of the Presence of God*; and *Truth vs Falsehood*. Dr. Hawkins was a prolific writer, lecturer, and teacher, affecting huge numbers of people around the world. His physical form died in 2012, and since then his wife, Susan, has kept his invaluable teachings alive. You can delve into the spiritual teachings and work of Dr. David Hawkins on his website: veritaspub.com.

MICHAEL JAMES

From an early age, Michael James was filled with questions, and at nineteen he began a worldwide search for the meaning of life. He traveled through many countries, and ended up in the Himalayas and India, visiting many holy places and various ashrams looking for the purpose and the meaning of life. Eventually he went to Tiruvannamalai in India, to the ashram of Ramana Maharshi, who had died decades earlier. He planned to stay a few days but ended up staying for twenty years. On his arrival Michael read Ramana's book *Who Am I?* and he knew he had finally found what he was looking for. He proceeded to learn the Indian language of Tamil so that he could translate Ramana Maharshi's teachings, which he did over the next twenty years. I first learned of Michael when I saw him being interviewed on Conscious TV. I immediately read his illuminating book, *Happiness and the Art of Being*, which encapsulates Ramana's teachings and is Michael's life's work. Visit Michael's website at happinessofbeing.com.

BYRON KATIE

In the midst of an ordinary American life—two marriages, three children, and a successful career—Byron Katie entered a ten-year-long downward spiral into depression, agoraphobia, self-loathing, and suicidal despair. In desperation, Katie checked herself into a halfway house, where she was to wake up a week or so later with all her depression and fear gone. In their place Katie found herself intoxicated with joy, which has remained with her ever since. What she realized was that when she believed her thoughts she suffered, but when she questioned them she didn't suffer, and that this is true for every human being. From her experience of self-realization, Katie developed four questions that became known as "The Work." Those teachings have gone on to free hundreds of thousands of people worldwide of suffering, and continue to do so. I have used Katie's teachings to question my own thoughts, and I have been fortunate enough to be present at several of Katie's talks where she used her four questions to liberate people from their beliefs. Katie's books include *Loving What Is*, *A Mind at Home with Itself*, *A Thousand Names for Joy*, *I Need Your Love—Is That True?*, *A Friendly Universe*, and for children, *Tiger-Tiger—Is It True?* and *The Four Questions.* You can find out more about the beautiful Byron Katie's teachings here: thework.com.

LOCH KELLY

Loch Kelly combines wisdom teachings, psychology, and neuroscience studies to help us live an awakened life. After a spiritual journey that included several traditions and teachers, Loch realized his true nature. In his teachings, Loch shares from his own experience, which has given him great joy, freedom, and love, and helps people awaken as the next natural stage of human development. His books are *Shift into Freedom* and *The Way of Effortless Mindfulness.* You will also find a wealth of teachings, retreats, online videos, and courses on Loch's website: lochkelly.org.

J. KRISHNAMURTI

The late J. Krishnamurti was born in India in 1895 and knew his true nature from the time he was a child. He is widely regarded as one of the greatest thinkers and religious teachers of all time. My ex-husband listened to Krishnamurti throughout our marriage, so I was exposed to his teachings for many years in my twenties and thirties. But it wasn't until my spiritual journey after The Secret that I returned to his teachings and was finally able to understand them. Many of the teachers featured in this book were influenced by Krishnamurti's teachings. Krishnamurti spent his entire adult life speaking throughout the world to large audiences and to individuals, including writers, scientists, philosophers, religious figures, and educators, about the need for a radical change in mankind. He was concerned with all humanity, and he held no nationality or belief, and belonged to no particular group or culture. Krishnamurti left a large body of literature in the form of public talks, writings, discussions with teachers and students, television and radio interviews, and letters. Many of these have been published as books, in over fifty languages, along with hundreds of audio and video recordings. For the treasure trove of Krishnamurti's teachings, go to jkrishnamurti.org.

DR. ROBERT LANZA, M.D.

Dr. Robert Lanza is considered one of the fathers of the field of applied stem cell biology. He has hundreds of publications and inventions and over thirty scientific books, including *Biocentrism*, in which Dr. Lanza provides a compelling argument for consciousness as the basis for the Universe, rather than consciousness simply being its by-product. If you are looking for a brilliant scientific perspective on the contents of this book, then *Biocentrism: How Life and Consciousness Are the Keys to Understanding the True Nature of the Universe* will have you riveted, and more than fulfill every question you might have. Dr. Lanza has received numerous awards, including *Time* magazine's Top 100 list of the most influential people in the world, and *Prospect* magazine's top 50 "World Thinkers." Dr. Lanza has been described as a genius and a renegade thinker, and has been likened to Einstein. For more on the brilliant Robert Lanza, M.D., visit robertlanza.com.

PETER LAWRY AND KALYANI LAWRY

Peter and Kalyani Lawry are Australians who reside in Melbourne (my hometown). After an intense spiritual journey spanning several years, and after traveling through India, Peter and Kalyani both realized their true nature. It's rare to have a husband and wife both self-realized, and it makes the meetings that the two of them hold in Melbourne very special. I had a life-changing afternoon with Peter and Kalyani when I visited Melbourne a few years ago, and I was also fortunate to have had some private phone sessions with Kalyani. Their books are *A Sprinkling of Jewels* and *Only That*, authored by Kalyani. You can discover more at nonduality.com.au.

LESTER LEVENSON

Lester Levenson, the legend. He was the living proof of what takes place in a diseased body when the light of the truth penetrates it. Lester used to say that "dis-ease in the body is disease in the mind." He has been an inspiration to thousands upon thousands of people, and his teachings have continued to inspire and free many from suffering well after the death of his form in the '90s. Lester's style of teaching is simple and therefore crystal clear, and for this reason his teachings will continue to wake people up for centuries to come. Lester's legacy includes his main core group of students who became self-realized and who are now teachers in their own right. One of those is Hale Dwoskin, who is the guardian of Lester's work, and it is with enormous gratitude to him that I share so many of Lester's simple and powerful teachings in this book. Lester's teachings have played an instrumental part in my life and continue to do so. The majority of Lester's quotes featured throughout this book were drawn from *Happiness Is Free*, volumes 1–5, by Lester Levenson and Hale Dwoskin. To find out more about this wonderful teacher, go to sedona.com.

FRANCIS LUCILLE

Francis Lucille, who was born in France, now lives in the United States. Francis realized his true nature at thirty years of age when he met his teacher, Jean Klein. It was Jean Klein's suggestion that Francis move to the United States to teach and to share the truth with others. Francis trained in physics at the renowned École Polytechnique in France, and so he is able to bring a clear scientific perspective to his teachings. He has helped countless people realize their true nature through his beautiful, clear, and precise teachings, including student Rupert Spira, who is also featured in this book. I have done several retreats with Francis in California, and have also had the great pleasure of spending many hours with him at his property. Francis holds retreats each year in Europe as well as the States, along with in-person meetings (most weekends) that are shared via live webcast. You can participate in these meetings no matter where you are and experience the welcoming presence of this wonderful teacher. Francis's books are *Truth Love Beauty*, *The Perfume of Silence*, and *Eternity Now*, and I have read each of them multiple times over. You can find a vast array of brilliant teachings from Francis's meetings and retreats on his website: advaitachannel.francislucille.com.

SHAKTI CATERINA MAGGI

Shakti Caterina Maggi has been teaching for the last nine years, after awakening in 2003. Since she started teaching, Shakti has been sharing the message of awakening to our true nature as One Consciousness. She is Italian, resides in Italy, and holds retreats and meetings in Europe and around the world, along with webinars online. Meetings are held in Italian, and some are in English. I first saw Shakti at a spiritual conference that I attended, where her talk and presence impacted me a lot. She is featured in the book *On the Mystery of Being*. She also writes a blog in English, and you can find many insightful articles on her website: shakticaterinamaggi.com.

RAMANA MAHARSHI

The late Ramana Maharshi is legendary. In 1896, at sixteen years of age, an intense fear of death came upon him. Ramana lay down and welcomed death completely. In that moment he transformed from being a person to what is actually real—the deathless Spirit. For Ramana, from that day on, the outward person that he seemed to be existed only in the view of others—in his view there was only the infinite space of awareness. Ramana's teachings reveal the direct path to awakening through self-inquiry, which is what is used by many of the teachers featured in this book. His teachings point you toward your innermost self, the only reality underlying all that exists. I am simply one of many whose lives have been transformed through Ramana Maharshi's teachings. To find out more about this legendary being, visit his website, where there is a wealth of books available to download for free: sriramanamaharshi.org.

MOOJI

Mooji was born in Jamaica and moved to London as a teenager. He now lives in Portugal, where he established Monte Sahaja, Centre for Self-Realisation. Mooji's spiritual awakening was sparked in 1987 through an encounter with a Christian mystic and culminated in 1993 at the feet of his master, the renowned Indian sage, Papaji. Since then, countless people have gone to Mooji seeking spiritual guidance, many coming to recognize their true nature. His profound teachings have developed a large following globally, especially on YouTube, where he makes many of his talks (satsangs) freely available as videos. Mooji's style of teaching resonates with many, in particular his sense of humor, analogies, storytelling, and metaphors, which he deftly uses to illuminate the truth. Like many others, I have watched hundreds of Mooji's talks online. I traveled to Portugal to attend one of Mooji's retreats with my daughter, and my daughter experienced her true self at that retreat. No endorsement could be greater than this. Mooji's books include *Vaster Than Sky, Greater Than Space*; *White Fire*, second edition; *The Mala of God*; and *An Invitation to Freedom* (a small but great book to realize your true self). You can find his books and an abundance of the teachings from this beautiful being at mooji.org.

MY TEACHER

My teacher, who wishes to remain anonymous, was a student of Lester Levenson and Robert Adams, who are two of my favorite teachers from the past. Four years ago, when I first met my teacher and stood in her presence, I was overcome with blissful joy. When you feel this level of bliss, you never want it to leave. This level of bliss is our true nature! Unfortunately, the blissful joy didn't stay permanently, because gradually my mind returned, bringing with it its unhappiness and stress. But with my teacher's guidance, following her practices religiously (all featured in this book), and being regularly in her presence, my mind became weaker and weaker. Now, peace and happiness are here with me most of the time, and I know it can be like this for everyone.

JAC O'KEEFFE

Jac O'Keeffe is Irish, and now based in Florida. Jac uncovered the truth and became self-realized over ten years ago. You can't ask for anything better than her teachings, where she pushes the boundaries of the conditioned mind. She is known for her clarity and direct manner, and she holds retreats, workshops, and private sessions for students. I discovered Jac online a few years ago, and I found her teachings to be like a breath of fresh air. I have also been fortunate to have attended some of her talks in person. You can be further inspired by Jac's work through her books *Born to Be Free* and *How to Be a Spiritual Rebel*. Like every teacher in this book, she is dedicating her life to freeing humanity from unnecessary suffering caused by the mind so we can live in the joyful happiness and bliss of our true self. Her website is jac-okeeffe.com.

MAX PLANCK

German physicist Max Planck made many contributions to theoretical physics, but his fame resulted primarily from his discovery of energy quanta, for which he won the Nobel Prize in 1918, and which revolutionized human understanding of atomic and subatomic processes.

SRI POONJA

Sri Poonja, affectionately known as "Papaji" by his students, one of whom was Mooji, was born in India. Papaji was drawn to spirituality when he was just a child, having his first spiritual experience at the age of nine. It would be some thirty years later that Papaji's spiritual search would end when he met Ramana Maharshi and realized his true self. During the '80s and '90s thousands upon thousands of people flocked to Lucknow in India to be with the energy of Papaji. He left his body in 1997. To discover more about Papaji's teachings, visit avadhuta.com.

ROSE CROSS ORDER

In the introduction and throughout the book I mention the Rose Cross Order, whose head office is based in the Canary Islands in Spain. I was made an honorary member of this nonprofit organization, which is dedicated to raising the consciousness of humanity. The formation of the Rose Cross Order in Europe dates back to the fourteenth century, but it is also the spiritual heir of the Ancient Schools of Knowledge that flourished in Babylon, Egypt, Greece, and Rome and, perhaps, even earlier. The Order has had many distinguished beings as members, who over the centuries worked silently and diligently, at great risk to themselves, to free humanity from their suffering with the truth. Francis Bacon was the Imperator of the Rose Cross Order during his life, Isaac Newton was a member, and they are just two of the many famous names associated with the Order. The current Imperator of the Order, Angel Martin Velayos, has mentored me over many years. I studied the Rose Cross teachings over a ten-year period, completing over twenty-two degrees of the English teachings, and they have had a huge impact in helping me see and understand the truth. For more about the Order, visit www.rosicrucian-order.com.

RUMI

Rumi was a thirteenth-century Sufi mystic and poet. Rumi's influence and poignant words of truth have transcended all borders of religion, geography, and spiritual tradition, and his poems continue to be treasured throughout the world.

PETER RUSSELL

Peter Russell, who originally trained in physics and mathematics at Cambridge University, has studied sciences and spiritual traditions throughout his life. Some of his many books are *The Global Brain*, *The TM Technique*, *Waking Up in Time*, *From Science to God*, and *The Consciousness Revolution*. I had the pleasure of seeing Peter speak at the Science and Nonduality Conference in San Jose. You can find many of his talks free of charge on his website, along with his extensive teachings: peterrussell.com.

SENECA

Lucius Annaeus Seneca (4 BC–AD 65) was a Roman philosopher and statesman. He is known for his writings, which include plays, prose works, essays, and letters.

RUPERT SPIRA

Rupert Spira is British and resides in England, where he holds regular meetings and retreats. Rupert also travels extensively to hold retreats in Europe and the United States multiple times each year. Originally an artist and ceramicist, after twenty years of spiritual practice and meditation, Rupert recognized his true nature through his teacher, Francis Lucille. Rupert's articulate and very intimate style of teaching has transformed the lives of a very large number of students. His teachings played an important part in my journey of awakening, especially in the disidentification from the body. Rupert's response to a student's question is to painstakingly ensure that the student actually experiences the answer to their question, rather than being given a mental concept as an answer. Many video and audio teachings from Rupert's retreats and talks are available on his website. Rupert's books, all of which I have read, are *The Nature of Consciousness; Transparent Body, Luminous World; The Light of Pure Knowing; The Transparency of Things; The Art of Peace and Happiness; The Intimacy of All Experience; Being Aware of Being Aware;* and *The Ashes of Love.* Visit rupertspira.com.

ECKHART TOLLE

Eckhart Tolle is a spiritual teacher and author, born in Germany. Eckhart had been depressed for most of his life, when at the age of twenty-nine he had a profound inner transformation that radically changed the course of his life. With his international bestsellers, *The Power of Now* and *A New Earth*—translated into over fifty-two languages, he has introduced millions to the joy and freedom of living life in the present moment. Eckhart's profound yet simple teachings have already helped countless people throughout the world find inner peace and greater fulfillment in their lives. At the core of his teachings is a spiritual awakening that he sees as the next step in human evolution. An essential aspect of this awakening is transcending our ego-based state of consciousness. Like many millions of other people, I first discovered Eckhart's teachings in his book *The Power of Now.* I had many shifts and spiritual experiences reading that book, and I carried *Practicing the Power of Now* with me and followed its practices for some years. His other books are *Stillness Speaks* and the children's books *Guardians of Being* and *Milton's Secret.* Eckhart holds retreats and gives talks all over the world, which results in an enormous contribution to humanity as he frees many from the binds of suffering caused by the ego. Eckhart's website is eckharttolle.com.

UPANISHADS

The Upanishads are ancient Sanskrit texts of spiritual teachings, written circa 800–200 BC. They are a part of the oldest spiritual scriptures of Hinduism, the Vedas.

ALAN WATTS

The late Alan Watts was a British writer and teacher who popularized Eastern philosophies for Western audiences. Beautifully spoken, Alan Watts's lectures continue to remain popular worldwide, many years after the death of his physical form in 1973. Alan wrote twenty-five books (many of which I have read). Among the most popular are *The Book: On the Taboo Against Knowing Who You Are*, *The Wisdom of Insecurity*, and *The Way of Zen*. His children have made several of his lectures available online as videos, and they have also preserved his talks and lectures on the Alan Watts website so that his contribution to the planet may continue for generations to come: alanwatts.org.

PAMELA WILSON

Pamela Wilson lives in the Bay Area of Northern California and was a student of Lester Levenson and Robert Adams. For over twenty years she has traveled throughout the United States, Canada, and Europe holding retreats and giving talks and private sessions in the nonduality tradition. She is sweetness and compassion itself, and I have been fortunate enough to attend several of her talks. She is also featured in the book *On the Mystery of Being*, from Science and Nonduality. For more on Pamela, her website contains an abundance of her teachings: pamelasatsang.com.

PARAMAHANSA YOGANANDA

In the more than one hundred years since his birth, this beloved world teacher has come to be recognized as one of the greatest emissaries to the West of India's ancient wisdom. Yogananda's life and teachings continue to be a source of light and inspiration to people of all races, cultures, and creeds. Among those who became his students were many prominent figures in science, business, and the arts, and he was officially received at the White House by President Calvin Coolidge. I first discovered Yogananda's teachings when, like so many others, I read *Autobiography of a Yogi*, a book that has sold millions of copies. It's an unforgettable book that sparked a spiritual revolution, and it had a profound effect on me as well. You can read *Autobiography of a Yogi* online on the website of the Self-Realization Fellowship (which Yogananda founded). Yogananda has many other books, and through subscription on their website you can receive the SRF Lessons written by Yogananda himself: yogananda.org.